Page to Stage

Page to Stage

Developing Writing, Speaking and Listening Skills in Primary Schools

James Carter

 **David Fulton** Publishers

This edition reprinted in 2010 by Routledge
2 Park Square, Milton Park, Abingdon, Oxon, OX14 4RN
Simultaneously published in the USA and Canada
By Routledge
270 Madison Avenue, New York, NY 10016

First published in Great Britain in 2005 by David Fulton Publishers

10 9 8 7 6 5

British Library Cataloguing in Publication Data
A catalogue record for this book is available from the British Library.

ISBN 978-1-84312-215-9

Designed and typeset by Kenneth Burnley, Wirral, Cheshire
Printed and bound in Great Britain

Contents

Acknowledgements

This book is dedicated to Jacqueline Wilson, Helen Fairlie and Brian Moses – thank you for all your amazing support and encouragement – as well as to Ian Beck and Mark Hawkins – thank you for all the time and talent that you have brought to this book as well as to my previous books/CDs.

Of all the others I need to thank I must start at home, with a planet of love for my three best friends: my fantastic wife Sarah, and our two lovely daughters, Lauren and Madeleine.

Big thanks to Caroline Royds, Paul Harrison and Mara Bergman at Walker Books for helping me to grow and develop some of my own poems included in this book.

Much gratitude to all those poets and authors who have allowed me to reproduce their quotes and workshops – including Brian Moses, Pie Corbett, Ian Beck, Tony Mitton, Valerie Bloom, Roger Stevens, Matthew Sweeney, Satoshi Kitamura, John Foster, Jan Dean, Russell Hoban, Berlie Doherty, Michael Rosen, Colin Macfarlane, Roger McGough, Benjamin Zephaniah, Kenneth Koch, Peter Cutts and Morris Gleitzman.

Other people who really deserve far more than just a thank you are Ian Brown and Ken Bentley.

Many, many thanks to these schools for allowing me to reproduce some of their poems:

Wolston St Margaret's C of E Primary, Wolston; Storrington First School, Storrington; Broadlands Primary School, Hereford; The Manor Prep School in Abingdon; RAF Benson Primary School, Oxfordshire; Freeland Primary School, Oxfordshire.

A very special thanks to Helen Clark and her staff at Dorchester St Birinus Primary School in Oxfordshire for inviting me in so many times and letting me try out a number of new workshops and for allowing me to include some of your school's poems.

And so much thanks to Wendy Jacobs, Penny Hollander and Class 4 at Ewelme (C of E) Primary School in Oxfordshire. First of all, thank you for letting Mark and me turn your classroom into a recording studio one afternoon just before SATs in early May 2004. Thank you to Penny and Wendy for preparing your class for the recording. (Mark said that I should mention that Ewelme School dates back to 1437 when it was set up by Dame Alice Chaucer and is the oldest school in England.) I also have to say that without Ewelme (C of E) Primary School much of the second part of this book and the accompanying CD would not have been possible. So thank you for your time, energy, enthusiasm, creativity and vitality – and of course talent.

The following poems are reproduced by permission of James Carter: 'Fuss Fuss Fuss or the Goldilocks Rap'; 'World of Weird'; 'Talking Time' (commissioned by Coral Arts); 'J.A.M.E.S.'; 'This is a Poem'; 'Sorry Sorry Sorry'; 'Jabberwhatty' (after 'Jabberwocky' by Lewis Carroll);

'Fizz'; 'Silver Planet Haiku'; 'Icy Morning Haiku'; 'Friendship Poem'; 'Shark'; 'Autumn'. From *Cars Stars Electric Guitars* © 2002 James Carter, reproduced by permission of Walker Books Ltd): 'Night Car Journey'; 'Shooting Stars'; 'Electric Guitars'; 'The Dark'. Extracts from: 'Scoff the Sky – A Day in the Life of a Chocoholic'; 'Love You More'; 'Red Cheese'; 'Animal Instincts'; 'Santa: Ace Guy or Strange Bloke?'; 'Write Your Name'; 'The A–Z of Bopping Birds'.

With special thanks to the following for allowing their work to be reproduced in this book. Valerie Bloom for 'The Visitor' (© Valerie Bloom 2003, from *Whoop an' Shout!*, published by MacMillan Children's Books, reprinted by permission of the author); Lewis Carroll for 'Jabberwocky'/extract from 'The Walrus and the Carpenter'/extract from 'A-Sitting on a Gate' (from *Alice's Adventures in Wonderland/Alice Through the Looking-Glass*); Helen Dunmore for 'Hedgehog Hiding at Harvest in Hills Above Monmouth' (originally published in *Snollygoster*. Copyright © Helen Dunmore 2001. All rights reserved. First published by Scholastic Children's Books and reproduced by permission of Scholastic Ltd); Paul Fleischman for 'Fireflies' (from *Poems for Two Voices* – HarperCollins; text copyright © 1988 Paul Fleischman. Used by permission of HarperCollins Publishers); John Foster for 'Grandma', © 1996 John Foster (from *You Little Monkey* (Oxford University Press), included by permission of the author); Katherine Gallagher for 'A Girl's Head' (© Kat herine Gallagher 2004, reprinted by permission of the author); Red Grammer for 'Places in the World' (from the recording *Teaching Peace*, ©1986 Smilin' Atcha Music, written by Red and Kathy Grammer, distributed through Red Note records, www.redgrammer.com); Edward Lear for two limericks; Tony Mitton for 'Anansi Meets Big Snake' (from *The Tale of Tales* – David Fickling Books); Harold Munro for 'Overheard on a Saltmarsh' (from *The Collected Works of Harold Munro*); Brian Patten for 'You Can't Be That' (from *Thawing Frozen Frogs* – Viking; copyright © 1989 Bernard Maclaverty. Reproduced by permission of the author, c/o Rogers, Coleridge & White Ltd, 20 Powis Mews, London W11 1JN); Michael Rosen for 'Straining' (from *Centrally Heated Knickers* – Puffin; reprinted by permission of PFT on behalf of Michael Rosen, © 2000 Michael Rosen); Kit Wright for 'Red Boots On' (from *The Bear Looked Over the Mountain* – Salamander Press); Berlie Doherty for the opening sentences from *Spellhorn* (Lions – HarperCollins); Russell Hoban for the opening sentence from *The Mouse & His Child* (Faber & Faber); J. K. Rowling for the opening sentence from *Harry Potter and the Philosopher's Stone* (Bloomsbury); William Shakespeare for extracts from the play *Macbeth*; 'Ananasi Meets Big Snake' by Tony Mitton, from *Tale of Tales*, published by David Fickling Books.

Additional texts referred to: *The Story of Tracy Beaker/The Dare Game/Double Act* by Jacqueline Wilson (Random House); the *Harry Potter* books by J. K. Rowling (Bloomsbury); *Kensuke's Kingdom* by Michael Morpurgo (HarperCollins); the novels of Anthony Horowitz (Walker Books); *Toy Story* and *Finding Nemo* (Disney/Pixar films).

Introduction

Aims of *Page to Stage*

The central aim of *Page to Stage* is to give teachers a wide range of practical activities for use in and out of the Literacy Hour. The activities in this book relate to writing as well as to speaking and listening, and can be put into immediate practice in the primary classroom. The two main parts of *Page to Stage* cover writing and performing poetry, and these two separate but interconnected parts can be used independently. The majority of the activities relating to writing and performing poetry in this book have been tried and tested in poetry writing workshops in primary classrooms all over the UK – and a great many of them have also been used in INSET sessions.

Why writing, and speaking and listening, together in one book? Well, the writing and then the sharing – call it speaking and listening or reading or performing – of a poem go naturally together. Having written poems, most children of primary age are keen to talk about and share their writing with their peers. On one level, *Page to Stage* explores and exploits the relationship between writing and speaking and listening, or the journey from literacy to oracy. But really, most writing in the classroom is part of a process or continuum that naturally begins and concludes with oracy:

Oracy (speaking and listening: brainstorming, discussing, formulating and sharing ideas) >

Literacy (writing: crafting and drafting) >

Oracy (speaking and listening: reading out, discussing, evaluating, rehearsing, performing)

Each section in the first part of *Page to Stage* provides models, templates and structures for children's poetry writing. Ideally, children should never be encouraged to go straight into a writing activity cold. As teachers we recognise the need for stimulating and nurturing the creative mind and well know that perfect, immaculate final drafts do not appear after 45 minutes of furious scratching away with pen and paper. Poems grow over a number of drafts. Much can change from initial idea through to final draft. An indifferent first draft of a poem – with much crafting and insight and guidance – can turn that piece into a very special final draft. But children need to know what to look for when they are developing their poems. For this very reason, there is a photocopiable sheet on p. 84 entitled 'Crafting and Drafting'.

The language throughout this book is kept as accessible and straightforward as possible. Most of the main sections within the book are directed at teachers, yet the language in the individual workshops is frequently written in the second person – using 'you' – and is aimed at children in the primary classroom, so that teachers can read out these sections directly to the class. Another aim of *Page to Stage* is to not weigh teachers down with too much technical poetic jargon, which can be off-putting and alienating. For this very reason, the 'Rhythm and Rhyme' section does not discuss such areas as meter or iambics; likewise, the

'Free Verse' section does not make mention of such issues as enjambement and caesura with reference to line breaks. Anyway, such areas are more frequently the preserve of Key Stages 3 and 4.

Most of the workshops are pitched somewhere between Years 2 and 6, but some activities may need modification for Year 1. Indeed, the ideas in *Page to Stage* are not set in stone, and teachers must feel free to adopt and adapt workshops according to class needs, interests and ability levels.

What's So Good About Poetry?

- Most poems are *short*, bite-size chunks of text, perfect for literacy activities – and even during in-between times throughout the day.
- Poems highlight the *musicality* of language, with aspects such as rhythm, rhyme and repetition.
- Poems are ideal for exploring aspects of *language* such as alliteration and assonance; imagery; and figurative language such as metaphor and simile.
- Poems often adopt other forms of *language*, such as conversations, adverts, letters and lists.
- Poems are in *many forms* – including free verse, haikus, kennings, rhyming verse – so are ideal for children exploring structures and modes of language.
- Poems cover a range of *subject matters* – and material can be fictional, factual, autobiographical and anecdotal.
- Poems can have a range of *tones* – from the lightweight and frivolous to the profound and spiritual.
- Poems are perfect for developing *speaking and listening skills* – for *discussing, analysing, debating, reflecting upon, sharing* – as well as for *learning* and ultimately *performing*.
- Poems are ideal for *displays* and for *publishing*.
- Poetry (especially free verse) is arguably the *ideal medium* for children to write about themselves – and to write about their own thoughts, emotions, memories and experiences.
- Poems can be written *anywhere* – in the playground, on school trips; farms, art galleries, museums, etc.
- Most of all, poetry is there for *enjoying*!

All the time spent working on poetry will inform, nourish and enrich all those skills related to other areas such as fiction and non-fiction. Poetry is not just a corner of literacy, it underpins all aspects of it.

A Poetry-Rich Classroom

Here are a few tips on how to ensure that a classroom is exploiting poetry to its full potential.

- Keep a *good supply of poetry books*, modern and traditional. A range of verse – haikus to raps, kennings to free verse – funny pieces to more serious pieces. Have a poetry box. Update the books: see what new books – anthologies and collections – are being published.
- *Poems on tape/CD* – listen to a whole variety of poems and poets, old and new.
- *Photocopy poems* – and enlarge them – put them up in unusual places. On doors, in corridors, even in the loos! Put up a whole range: from shape poems to acrostics to raps to free verse.

- *Poem of the week* – display the children's own poems in a set place, say a board in the classroom or the noticeboard at the front of the school. Rotate weekly. Do this all year round. Have weekly poem topics – there are poems on every subject under, above and including the sun!
- *Poem of the day* – just after register every day a child reads out a favourite poem.
- *Poet of the week* – reading poems by one chosen poet, e.g. Allan Ahlberg or Michael Rosen.
- *Poetry tree* – with favourite poems and poets.
- *Poetry concerts/assemblies* – children perform poems they have written, and perform either as individuals, in groups or as a whole class.
- *Forms of poems* – display, showing examples of the most common forms of poems, from free verse to acrostics to shape poems, etc. Examples can be regularly changed.
- *Publish poems* regularly – in class anthologies, on the school website, at poetry websites (e.g. Poetryzone: www.poetryzone.com; Man in the Moon website: www.maninthemoon.co.uk), and entering competitions (e.g. the Poetry Society).

Clearly, not every teacher likes poetry, but every teacher will find some poems that they enjoy and will want to share with their class. Rather than 'We did poetry last term' – how about 'Poetry? We do a little bit every day!'

Children need to be encouraged to *read* as *writers* – to actively digest and analyse poems that can teach them a range of poetic devices and conventions and structures that they can use in their own writing. But also, children need to write as readers – to learn how to write poems that will entertain, surprise and stimulate them – all of which takes much experience and practice. What follows is a book dedicated to developing these very skills.

Page

Developing *writing* skills through poetry

The Writing Process and Poetry Writing Workshop Structure

Poetry workshops – or any other form of writing workshops – need to follow a coherent structure to enable the mind to create effectively, to give children time to mull over ideas, to share ideas and for the resulting material to fully grow and develop. Here is one such structure that can easily be adapted or modified:

- *Thinking time:* being given a short while to consider the topic/focus/stimuli. Children need to work in such a way that encourages creative thinking – not actively and consciously wondering 'What shall I write? What can my poem be about?, but more a kind of daydreaming state where the mind wanders and wonders, can be creative and play with potential ideas for writing.

  As Ted Hughes advocates in his seminal book *Poetry in the Making*, it is essential not to rush into writing a poem. Hughes says that time spent thinking, pondering and mentally exploring is vital – and integral to the creative process. To commit an idea to paper too early can quash an idea before it is fully realised.
- *Talking time:* time to talk, discuss, to listen to and to share ideas either as a whole class or in small groups – which can also be part of:
- *Brainstorming time:* listing all ideas – everything that comes to mind. At this point it is vital to emphasise that *all* ideas are worth putting down, as you cannot tell which ones will be used at a later stage. Teachers can act as scribe for some of the children's ideas, but children can produce their own brainstorms as well prior to writing. Children can also share and discuss their ideas with a partner.
- *Writing time:* this can happen at various stages – from the first draft, to further revisions and edits on to the final draft.
- *Sharing time:* time to read out and share with the class, for others to comment and feed back and for children to reflect upon their own poems – saying how effective they feel the poem is and what aspects may need further work.

These stages can be recursive. Having written a poem, a child can read out a first draft, share comments from others, and go back to more writing – and so it goes on.

Children will create in different ways. They need to be able to discover how they function best with writing, and be able to explore their own creative process – and understand how they function best as a writer. The older and more confident children become with their writing, the more they need to be given scope to follow their own creative paths in workshops. To show how one set workshop can lead off into various directions, there are three very different children's poems included in this book that all stem from the same workshop. These are 'Owls' (p. 31), 'Twinkling Twilight' (p. 30) and 'Magic in the Moonlight – a Midnight Mystery' (p. 127) (track 7 on CD).

Confidence with Writing Poetry

There's that old saying that we have all got a book within us. Is it true? Maybe it is. But one thing for sure is that everyone is capable of writing at least a handful of really fine poems. It's all a question of nurturing the skills, instilling a love and respect for language; but above all, it is a matter of developing confidence.

Confidence comes from being given regular opportunities to write creatively – from our imaginations as well as from our own experiences. As the novelist/poet Berlie Doherty says, 'Writing is the combination of *I remember* and *Let's pretend*.' Confidence in writing is when children are feeling positive about exploring their ideas, and feeling comfortable enough to write down any thoughts, words or images that come to them as they are brainstorming. As a writer you never know what ideas you are going to use at a later stage, so you have to be prepared to write down literally anything that comes to mind. In the classroom this can only be achieved if (a) children have no inhibitions, and (b) they are concentrating on the creative rather than the formal aspects of writing (handwriting, spelling, punctuation and grammar), which can be properly addressed at a later editing stage. Above all, children's confidence comes from feeling that their ideas and their writing are of value and that they as writers are respected by the classroom teacher – which can further be achieved by having their work regularly published.

Confidence can also come as a result of having positive feedback to writing. The poet Brian Moses has a most effective way of encouraging children to develop their poems. In a workshop, when a child reads out, Brian will first listen and then respond with a compliment – something like, 'You have a great title/opening line there' and then he will make a suggestion for improvement; perhaps, 'but the rhythm of the second line doesn't quite flow yet. Could you shorten that line?' And it is always good to ask a child what they think about your response: 'Do you agree?' 'What do you think?'

For children to become confident and competent language-users, they need to be able to express themselves in their own voices (see 'Free Verse' section). As noted earlier, poetry is perhaps the best medium for children to write about their worlds, their memories, their life experiences, their families and friendships, things that matter to them and everything around them. Children need to be given experience of using a range of poetic forms so that ultimately they can choose the most appropriate mode of expression – be it a rhyming piece, a free verse poem, a kenning or a list poem, or whatever. We need to build up children's poetic repertoires so that they have the ability to select the medium/mode that best befits want they want to say. And within the various forms, children can use their own voices, dialects and language particular to their home, culture and religion. Just because they are writing poetry doesn't mean that everything has to be figurative or metaphoric. The voice can be contemporary and colloquial.

Children need to be aware that every idea is good in the right place. When brainstoming ideas or writing a first draft, children need to be reassured that there is no such thing as a bad or wrong idea. Every idea is good (a) in the appropriate place, and (b) with work. But it can take time to decide which ideas to use and how to develop them (see Crafting and Drafting photocopy sheet on p. 84). When conducting workshops, the educationalist/ author Steve Bowkett, on hearing a child give an idea that cannot be used directly in the evolving piece of writing on the board, will tell the child that s/he has a 'little treasure' to put in their pocket to bring out later when they are doing their own piece of writing. What a wonderfully reassuring thing to say!

In workshops, children frequently ask such questions as, 'Is this right?' or 'Am I allowed to do this . . . ?' as if poetry – like grammar or punctuation – has a strict, rigid set of rules and regulations. Children need to be told regularly that they are in charge of their poems, that it is not a case of right and wrong – but writing is something that they should enjoy, something to be pleased with.

As fanciful as it may sound, poetry is, in a number of ways, like jazz. Of all the written language forms, poetry is the most playful, adventurous, experimental, subversive and, of course, rhythmical and melodic. Children need to experience all of these qualities that poetry can have. Children need to discover in their own writing the playfulness of words and feel confident enough to explore language – to stretch themselves, to find new ways of wording what they want to say. They need to take risks, to challenge their own notions of poetry and what they can and can't do. They need to shock, surprise and delight themselves, to push the boundaries of what they are capable of and what a poem is. What is better than a child holding up a piece of paper and telling you, 'Wow! I never thought I could do that!' Or 'I really like what I've just written!' It happens. One B.Ed. undergraduate at Reading University, when asked for a definition of poetry, said, 'Anything goes.' How liberating an approach that is. We need children to feel liberated in their writing too.

Children do not produce perfect poems every time they sit down and write a poem. Many pieces won't work at all. Professional writers often find this too: many pieces are non-starters. As the children's author and poet Russell Hoban has said, process is as important as product. And for this reason not every poem or piece of writing should be crafted and drafted. Sometimes, if something isn't working, it is best to move on to something else.

The other important aspect of confidence with regard to poetry is that of reading and performing poems. This area is covered in the second part of this book.

Role(s) of the Teacher

Teachers have various roles to play in relation to writing poetry in the classroom:

- as *model* of creative writing – someone who co-creates with the class, acts as scribe for children's creativity, shares their own writing and talks about their own creative processes;
- as *reader* and *performer* of poetry – a model that children can listen to, follow and emulate;
- as *initiator* of a variety of poetry-writing activities – covering a range of poetic forms and using a variety of different stimuli (music, images, artefacts, model poems);
- as *editor* of the children's writing – guiding their creativity and helping them to develop as writers;
- as *publisher* of children's writing;
- and above all – as *motivator*!

Publishing

Publishing helps to give a purpose, a direction, a goal as well as a reward to writing. Above all, it increases children's motivation and helps boost self-esteem. Young writers need to see that there is a product as well as a process to their writing – which can be published in a variety of ways, including:

- class/year group/school *anthologies* – as themed or miscellaneous anthologies;
- *displays* – in the classroom, the classroom windows/door, in the corridors, in the hall, at the entrance to the school, or as 'poem/story of the week' on notice boards;
- poems can be *recorded* onto audio cassette or video; likewise, performances of poems – perhaps to coincide with a visiting writer – can also be recorded in this way;
- poems can be read/*performed* to other year groups;
- *local media* – newspapers/radio stations, who may be happy to broadcast recordings done by the school or may invite pupils to record poems/stories in their studios;

- the *school website* and other *websites*
    - 'Poetryzone' – www.poetryzone@ndirect.co.uk
    - Young ABC Tales – www.youngABCtales.com
    - The Poetry Society – tel. 020 7420 9880 – www.poetrysoc.com – and *The Times Educational Supplement* both run writing competitions.

Finding and Keeping Ideas

As Bob Dylan – who many claim is our greatest living poet – has said, ideas are everywhere, you can just pluck them out of the air. Children often ask poets, 'Where do you get your ideas from?' and John Foster's own response – 'a mixture of experience, observation and imagination' – has a useful message for children in that they need to be aware that ideas are all around them – in their lives, their memories, what they do, what they read and what they observe in the world. And really, it's not so much *what* you write about, but *how* you write about it. Anything is potentially good material for writing!

As the award-winning illustrator and author Ian Beck says:

> An idea never arrives perfectly formed. It has to be built upon. It will arrive as a nudge saying, 'You think about that.' And your instinct just tells you that this idea is worth thinking about.

And because of this, it is good for children to make a note of the idea and keep it stored in a notebook or a folder, in which they can collect and source all their ideas and any potential material for their poems.

Children's own mini-whiteboards are ideal for the first stage of the creative writing process. There is something very reassuring to a child about writing down ideas onto a whiteboard, and not having to make the same kind of commitment that comes with pen and paper. This 'taking the pressure off' often leads to greater creativity and a more relaxed workshop atmosphere. However, children must be encouraged not to wipe off any ideas, and to move on to paper by the end of the session – otherwise, teachers can spend valuable break times photocopying the boards!

More and more, children are given opportunities to write poems on computers. John Foster has this advice for those who do:

> I suggest to children that if they use a computer they should do lots of printouts. I recommend that they don't use the 'Delete' button too often and I advise that they type out all the different versions as they go along so that they can keep all of their ideas. I write my poems by hand, and I do all my drafts on one single sheet of paper. This enables me to use words or phrases or lines that I might have crossed out in an earlier draft of a poem. This way, I don't ever lose any of my ideas. More of my poems are written by hand than on a computer – but that's because the idea will come when I'm away from the screen. I don't find sitting in front of the screen conducive to finding ideas for poems.

Ways Into Writing Poetry

There are many ways of approaching the writing of poems – and all are equally appropriate and effective. These methods are not mutually exclusive – poetry-writing approaches often overlap. Yet all of these methods will inevitably require teachers either to act at times as scribe or to brainstorm ideas on the board prior to children writing themselves.

- Use *specific poems* as models – popular Key Stage 2 poems include 'The Sound Collector' by Roger McGough, 'The Magic Box' by Kit Wright, 'Down Behind the Dustbin' by Michael Rosen and 'Ten Things Found in a Wizard's Pocket' by Ian McMillan (see 'Free Verse', 'Rhythm and Rhyme' and 'Image and Metaphor' sections for some model poems).
- Write *communal poems* – teacher acts as scribe at the board, while the children are sharing ideas and creating poems as a community of writers; the class can write to a set title or opening line/verse (see 'Free Verse': 'Starting Points') – this method can be done with any form of poem from raps to haikus to kennings.
- Write *autobiographical* poems – children drawing upon their own lives for source material. Teachers can focus on specific *themes* (see 'Themes' below and 'Free Verse': 'Autobiographical Writing').
- Look at *themes* as starting points for poems – themes that the children have experience of in their own lives, such as dreams, memories, journeys, school life, friends and family (see 'Free Verse': 'Autobiographical Writing').
- Explore the various *forms of poetry* – writing in a variety of poetic forms: free verse, rhyming poems, raps, kennings, shape poems, list poems, haikus (see 'Photocopiable Pages': 'Forms of Poetry').
- Use a range of *stimuli* to generate ideas for poetry writing – stimuli such as images (photos, paintings, illustrations), music (film soundtracks, instrumental music of all genres, songs and song lyrics), personal items brought in by the children, artefacts (of cultural or historical significance).
- Hone in on *poetic elements* – and doing exercises involving metaphor, simile, rhyme, rhythm, syllables, alliteration, assonance, onomatopoeia, point of view, writing in the first/second/third person, etc. (see 'Free Verse'; 'Rhythm and Rhyme' and 'Image and Metaphor' sections).

Using poems as models seems to be the most prevalent methodology for writing poetry – and is a very effective way of getting children to learn a variety of poetic patterns and structures. But it is not the only method. As valuable as it is, it does not always allow for children's poetic and creative voices to come through. Children need ultimately to write poems choosing the poetic form most suitable for their ideas. For example, an amusing anecdote might work well as a poem in rhyming couplets, an image of an autumn sunset could work well as a haiku, and an early childhood memory as a free verse piece.

By writing with stimuli such as music or images (see pp. 64 & 66), children will more easily and more freely be able to choose. Poetry is a generic term that covers a multiplicity of forms and therefore children need to have experience of a wide variety of these forms. Ideally, teachers will incorporate a range of approaches to writing poetry into their teaching methods.

1

Poetry Writing Warm-up Workshops

Creative writing comes far more easily if the brain has had a chance to prepare itself with a quick warm-up activity. The activity does not necessarily have to relate directly to the main workshop, and can simply be a fun literacy-centred introduction. What's more, warm-ups can provide some great ideas or starting points for poems.

The following activities can be done at the start of a longer writing session, or as short exercises in their own right – or even as stop-gap sessions. These activities can be done on paper or on children's mini-whiteboards.

Further exercises throughout this book that can be used as short warm-up activities:

- 'Down Behind the Dustbin' (p. 42)
- 'Sorry Sorry Sorry' (p. 42)
- 'My name is . . .' (p. 43)
- Chopping up prose (p. 21)
- New similes (p. 55)

Alliteration Competition

Write the longest possible sentence you can using only words that begin with the same letter. For example, 'A'. One opening phrase could be:

'Angry Arthur always ate . . .' – or you can think of your own.

Useful words when doing 'A' alliteration are 'also' and 'and'.

You can do this with any letter of the alphabet, and it does not need to make any sense at all.

Why not move down the alphabet – and create some fun tongue twisters:

Letter 'B': Brave Brian Brown brought Brainy Brenda bright brown bricks.

Letter 'D': Donald Donaldson didn't dare dive down deep.

Letter 'T': Tina Thomas talked to ten tiny toucans timidly . . .

Three-Word Poems

Write some fun alliterating three-word poems made up of a noun/a verb/an adverb:

Pandas pounce proudly.

Frogs fight fearlessly.

Samantha smiled sweetly.

Or – do an animal alphabet version

Ants amble athletically.

Badgers burrow brilliantly.

Crows caw creatively.

– and so on

Quick Class Poems 1

'I used to . . . but now I . . .' This quick activity was devised by the American poet Kenneth Koch. Everyone in the class completes the phrases:

I used to . . .
but now I . . .

– and can do one or two each. When finished, the whole class reads out in turn. Examples may include 'I used to crawl, but now I can walk.' Or 'I used to sink, but now I can crawl and do the butterfly and back stroke!' Other ways of doing this activity include (a) to try 'I used to have . . .' – for example, 'I used to have a box of holes – but now I have a bag of stars.' And (b) 'I used to be . . .', for example, 'I used to be a mountain of fears – but now I am a sea of calm.'

Quick Class Poem 2

This activity was devised by the poet Pie Corbett:

> I don't like . . .
> but I do love. . . .

Examples:

> I don't like the colour red, but I do love tomato soup.
> I don't like fire, but I love the flickering flame of a candle.

Ask the Impossible

Write a list of impossible questions and ask a friend or partner to reply to them with impossible answers. Examples:

> How much does the earth weigh?
> *Less than the sun but more than the moon*

> How cunning is a fox?
> *As cunning as a goldfish is forgetful.*

Daisy Chain

Write a sentence in which the last letter of every word is the same as the first letter of the following word. Examples:

> The egg grew wobbly yesterday, you understand.

> Kim met Tom – Mondays, Saturdays – secretly.

Mid-Line Acrostics

Write an autobiographical acrostic of your name (first name and surname if you wish) – but the key letters can only appear *during* the line – for example:

> My name is **J**ames
> I was born on **a** Thursday
> one Nove**m**ber
> in the y**e**ar 1959
> in a ho**s**pital

Rhyming Names

Write your own quick rhymes using first names. These two verses are inspired by John Foster's poem 'Brothers and Sisters' (*You Little Monkey!* – Oxford University Press).

> I've got a friend
> her name is Ruth
> she loves to wiggle
> her wobbly tooth

> I've got a friend
> his name is Sam
> his favourite food
> is strawberry jam

Do your own verses beginning:

> I've got a friend
> his/her name is . . .

2

Free Verse

Free verse is a very liberating form for young poets, and for a number of reasons. It is close in structure and language to human speech and is free from the constraints of meter, rhyme or set syllables. Like no other form of poetry, it lets the words breathe – both on the page and in performance. Free verse is the best form of poetry for children wanting to write about their own thoughts, reflections, memories and experiences.

Without doubt, the greatest pioneer of free verse poetry for children is Michael Rosen. It is well worth looking at some of his excellent poetry collections, such as *Wouldn't You Like to Know*, *Centrally Heated Knickers*, *Mind Your Own Business* and *Don't Put Mustard in the Custard*. Rosen's teacher's book, *Did I Hear You Write?* in which he talks about running writing free verse workshops in schools, is a 'must read' as well. One of Michael Rosen's free verse poems, 'Straining', is on p. 19.

Have a look at the range of other free verse poems in this book – 'Night Car Journey' (p. 15), 'Hedgehog Hiding at Harvest Above Monmouth Hills' (p. 49), 'A Girl's Head' (p. 18), 'The Shooting Stars' (p. 96), 'This is a Poem' (p. 20), 'Overheard on a Saltmarsh' (p. 116). Many free verse poems create their own structures. 'Hedgehog Hiding' on p. 49. has a list-poem type structure, using the phrase 'where you hide' to begin each verse. See how in the poem 'A Girl's Head' on p. 18 each verse has three lines and many verses begin with either 'There is' or 'There are'; these devices are useful for giving a shape and pattern to the poem. And the poem 'This is a Poem' shows that there are many ways of arranging words, phrases and lines.

Not everyone values free verse, and some claim it is just 'chopped-up prose'. But does it matter if it is? Why can't the boundaries between poetry and prose be blurred? Anyway, most free verse is distinctly different from prose – and uses such poetic devices as line breaks, alliteration, assonance and repetition as well as internal rhymes to provide extra music, texture and rhythm to the poem.

For the first six or seven years of children's lives we give them a healthy dose of nursery rhymes, lullabies and rhythmical rhyming poems. Then at some point in Year 2 or 3 we start telling children that there is a lot of poetry that doesn't rhyme. So we shouldn't be surprised to hear the response 'Oh yeah?' or come across some initial reluctance to write poetry such as free verse. Because of this, children need to see, read, perform and enjoy free verse poetry as much as possible prior to writing in this significant poetic form. A display in the classroom of the varying forms of free verse can be an effective way of exposing children to free verse on an ongoing basis.

Here are a few things to consider when writing free verse poems:

As with all forms of poetry, divide the poem into verses – unless the poem is very short. This way, it makes it both easier to write and to read and gives the words more space.

Use metaphoric language to colour your language and develop your imagery – similes and metaphors and personification – as well as onomatopoeia (sound words) and even calligrams, if you wish.

Keep the lines quite short – so that they are easy to read. Perhaps each line could be a short phrase:

> That night
> we went out in the dark
> and saw the shooting stars
> was one of the best nights ever
>
> (from 'The Shooting Stars' by James Carter)

If you have long lines, your poem will start to look and feel like prose.

A very valuable exercise in free verse – used in both children's and adult's poetry writing classes – is that of taking a sentence or short paragraph of prose and adapting it into a poem. One such workshop is featured in 'Free Verse: Chopping Up Prose'.

Step the lines if you want to:

> out into the world
> with tender
>   loving
>   care
>
> (from 'Take a Poem' by James Carter)

Stepping the lines slows the poem down and means that the reader will think more about individual phrases and words. Stepping works especially well at the end of a poem.

Free verse has rhythm too – but it is subtle, and is not as obvious as in rhyming poetry. The rhythm in free verse poetry is dictated by a number of factors – including the length of the lines, where the line breaks fall, as well as the use of repetition, alliteration, assonance, consonance and even internal rhyme. For repetition, see Helen Dunmore's 'Hedgehog Hiding in Hills Above Monmouth' and Katherine Gallagher's 'A Girl's Head'. The rhythm of free verse is like speech – to make it pleasing to the ear and easy to read and perform.

Think about where to use line breaks – the line breaks affect the flow of the poem and tell the reader where to take pauses. As the poet John Foster says:

> [Writing free verse is] all about developing the skill of knowing where to end each line and start a new one. There are two basic rules of thumb. One is to follow the patterns or phrasing of speech – and to pause where there is a natural break in speech. The other is to pause where there is a grammatical pause – and these two are not by any means the same. Speech is utterance, whereas writing conforms to grammatical rules. It can depend if someone is speaking in the poem or not – if they are, you follow the phrasing of speech.

Use dialogue. If you are writing about a true story – such as something that happened to you – speech will help to bring your poem to life and to give it extra vitality.

> Once
> my brother
> wanted to know why
> some cheese has got
> that red skin
> around it.

'Ah.' I said.
'Well.' I said.
'Are you really sure
you want to know this?' I said.
'Yes.' he said.

(from 'Red Cheese' by James Carter)

Also see 'Overheard on a Saltmarsh', p. 116.

Read it out loud as you write. This will help you to feel the rhythm of the poem, to decide where to end your lines and verses. Ask a friend to read it to you as well.

Night Car Journey

I wake up
sitting in the back seat
not quite sure
if it's real or a dream

and I look up
out through the darkness
out through the silence
to an infinite sky

and the moon bobs
in and out of treetops
turning the world
a ghostly blue

and my eyes
are heavy now
my eyes
are heavy now
my

James Carter

First draft of 'Night Car Journey', written by hand onto notepaper

Night
~~Long~~ Car Journey

I wake up
sitting in the back seat
not quite sure
if it's real or a dream

And I look ~~out~~ UP
out through the ~~window~~ darkness
out through the silence
to ~~the night going past~~ an infinite sky

And the moon bobs
in and out of tree tops
~~in between the buildings~~
and turns the ~~darkness~~ world
silvery blue

~~And the dark
is silver with the moon
and the night
is silent with the moon
And~~ my eyes
are heavy
my eyes are heavy
my eyes

Second/third drafts: second draft was typed onto computer and changes were made;
third draft was printed onto paper, where more changes were made. Final version (p. 15) is the fourth draft

A Girl's Head

(after the poem 'A Boy's Head' by Miroslav Holub)

In it there is a dream
that was started
before she was born,

and there is a globe
with hemispheres
which shall be happy.

There is her own spacecraft,
a chosen dress
and pictures of her friends.

There are shining rings
and a maze of mirrors.

There is a diary
for surprise occasions.

There is a horse springing hooves
across the sky.

There is a sea that
tides and swells
and cannot be mapped.

There is untold hope
in that no equation exactly
fits a head.

Katherine Gallagher

Straining

Dad was straining the potatoes
when he said to me:
Ssssh!
Don't tell anyone:
Some of the spuds have fallen out of the colander
and into the sink.
I've put the ones that fell out
back in with the others.
No one'll notice.
Ssssh!
Don't tell anyone.

So I didn't tell anyone.
And he was right.
No one noticed.
No one at all.
He got away with it.
Brilliant.

One problem:
my potatoes
tasted of washing up.

Thanks, Dad.

Michael Rosen

This
is a poem

a free verse poem
and
   the
      thing
        about
poems like
   these
is that
   they   come
in all SHAPES &
     SiZes

long lines like these are good if you want your reader to read quite quickly
whereas
      stepped lines
         like these
            are good
               for slowing
                  the reader
                    right d
                         o
                           w
                            n

as
are
thin
ones

But there are no set rules: you make your own.

Youcanevenjoinwordstogether   or set   them   apart.

YOU CAN USE BIG WORDS LIKE THESE FOR LOUD & BOLD THINGS

<small>or little words like these that seem to whisper</small>

In free verse poems you can use full stops. And commas, but you don't have to

         So
        do just
       ɹǝʌǝʇɐɥʍ
      seems and feels
     right for each poem!

James Carter (after Michael Rosen)

Chopping Up Prose

This exercise is a useful way of asking children to consider line breaks and stanzas in free verse. The text that follows is a paragraph of prose, which can be written on the board. The text will now be rewritten to look and feel as if it is a free verse poem. Punctuation such as commas and full stops can be taken out, or additional punctuation can be included. There is no right or wrong way of doing line breaks. It is at the discretion of each poet as to how they decide to form and structure their lines.

Here is the opening line from the first *Harry Potter* book by J. K. Rowling (Bloomsbury):

> Mr and Mrs Dursley, of number four, Privet Drive, were proud to say that they were perfectly normal, thank you very much.

Here is one way of representing the sentence above as a poem.

```
Mr and Mrs
Dursley
of number four
                Privet Drive
were PROUD
            to say
                    that they
were yltcefrep ˥∀ɯᴚON
thank
      you
          very
              much
```

Here it is again with commentaries:

Mr and Mrs	(nice alliterative phrase – and begs the question 'Mrs and Mrs who?)
Dursley	(by being a word on its own it highlights what a wonderfully horrible name it is!)
of number four	
Privet Drive	(stepped line, with near alliteration – 'pr' and 'dr')
were PROUD	(this is a 'calligram')
to say	(internal rhyme with 'they' below)
that they	(more alliteration and stepped line brings out rhythm)
were yltcefrep ˥∀ɯᴚON	(shows that they are not normal)
thank	
you	
very	
much	(four staccato steps to nicely finish off the poem)

It needs to be stressed that shorter lines are more effective in free verse as they (a) allow the reader to enjoy and focus on every word, and (b) look less like prose.

The important rules with this are that you can't change the words, or add any or take any away. In workshops, some children rearrange the words into a shape poem – Harry Potter's face or scar, a magic wand, a wizard's hat, the number four, the Dursleys' house and even a map of Privet Drive.

Choose lines from books you have been reading in class, to represent as free verse – or even as shape poetry.

Here are two short extracts from popular novels that can be chopped up into free verse:

The Watcher on the Hill

Night is falling. Far down in the valley warm house lights begin to glow. People come home from work and close their doors behind them. To the watcher on the hill the scene is strange.

(from Chapter 1 of *Spellhorn* by Berlie Doherty)

The tramp was big and squarely built, and he walked with the rolling stride of the long road, his steps too big for the little streets of the little town.

(from Chapter 1 of *The Mouse and his Child* by Russell Hoban)

Four Model Poems

The four workshops that follow are in free verse, non-rhyming forms that have repeated lines to give a pattern and structure to the pieces.

1: The Colourful Corridor

This activity can be done with classes from Year 1 upwards to Year 8 or 9. As with all the other workshops in the book, it can be adapted to individual interests, needs and ability levels. One standard way is to write this opening stanza on the board:

Down the white corridor
are many coloured doors

From here, each verse can begin:

Behind the . . . door.

At this point, the class can suggest some colours, and even other details such as sound and appearance.

Do a brainstorm of colours first and then make a list of doors.

Behind the *creaky brown* door.
Behind the *battered green* door.
Behind the *cobwebby cream* door.

Ask for volunteers to suggest what might be behind a creaky brown or battered green door. The point is to write a verse which really brings to life the worlds behind each door, using the most expressive language. It is vital with this activity to '*show*' and not '*tell*'. For instance,

Behind the black door
I saw a scary monster

is '*telling*' and will have no impact on the reader. But
Behind the black door
I heard a creature howling, growling and wailing

leaves more to the reader's imagination and is much more powerful.

Further issues to consider:

- The five senses are very useful as a guide. For instance, behind the blue door something could be seen, behind the rainbow door something could be tasted, behind the red door something could be touched. (See 'Five Senses', p. 59). In addition, the emotions, can be employed: 'Behind the brown door/I was horrified to discover . . .' 'Behind the white door/I was amazed to watch . . .'
- List the various things that doors are made of: glass, wood, metal and so on. So you could create a 'frosted glass door' or a 'rusty iron door' and so on.
- Less is more. Be subtle and give your reader little clues as to what might be behind a door, without making it too obvious. So, rather than 'Behind the chocolate brown door' try 'Behind the bubbly brown door/I feasted on a mountain of Mars Bars . . .'

Teachers can write a number of stanzas with the class, and the children from there could either write a couple of stanzas each (to contribute to a huge class poem) or a corridor poem of their own.

This poem can be adapted for a specific topic:

> Down the *Christmas* corridor
> are many coloured doors
>
> Behind the *gold* door
> the jangling and clanging of bells

Or:

> Down the *Egyptian* corridor
> are many coloured doors
>
> Behind the *yellow* door
> a lizard scitters
> across the desert sands

Alternatively – do a variety of doors from various times and places:

> Behind the castle door/pyramid door/spacecraft door . . .

Year 5 and 6 classes that have studied a variety of poetic forms could use a model that encourages children to write in different forms of poetry for each stanza:

> Down the poetry corridor
> are many coloured doors
>
> Behind the *bamboo* door:
> a small ted panda
> clings to the bars of the cage
> remembering home
>
> (a haiku poem)
>
>
> Behind the *graffiti* door
> an MC is rapping:
>
> *Brothers and sisters in da hood*
> *listen hard and listen good . . .*
>
> (a rap)

See other 'Forms of Poetry' on p. 78.

First brainstorm the colours, then discuss what might be behind the door and then choose which poetic form would best suit the subject matter.

Think of your own title for the poem. Here are some that children have come up with in various workshops: 'Doors Galore!', 'Mysterious Doors' and 'Pick a Door'.

'The Colourful Corridor' workshop is based upon the poem 'The Doors' by Philip Gross from the superb collection *Manifold Manor* (Faber & Faber).

The following abridged poem – using the 'Colourful Corridor' template – was written by Year 4 pupils at Manor Preparatory School in Abingdon on National Poetry Day 2003. The first two stanzas were composed by the whole class:

Dazzling Doors

Down the white corridor
are many coloured doors

Behind the jet black door
I heard a warty witch cackling
as she stirred her bubbling cauldron

Behind the aquamarine door
I weaved through the waves
on a dolphin's back
while the turtles paddled behind

Behind the moss green door
a huge jungle roared
with terrifying tigers and black-coated jaguars
emerging with menacing howls
from the dense green foliage

(Emma Walsh)

Behind the electric green door
hid the monsters of tomorrow
I heard them squelch and squish
in the green gunge of evolution

(Elizabeth Grant)

Behind the sky blue door
I felt soft cotton clouds of dreaming sheep
floating flimsily through the sun-streaked sky

(Mai Ito)

. . . And then just behind the cream door
I see
comforting
quiet
peaceful
H
O
M
E

(Elizabeth Wenninger)

2: The Magical Cat

This workshop is a variation on one devised by the poet Brian Moses, and was originally based on the poem 'The Magical Mouse' by the American poet Brian Patchen. The original poem can be found in Brian Patten's anthology *The Puffin Book of Twentieth Century Children's Verse*. The workshop can used with KS1 as well as KS2.

First the class brainstorm what cats do:

> Cats: eat/drink/walk/pounce/meow/purr/chase mice/are scared of dogs/lick themselves/sleep . . .

Teachers write out this introduction:

> **The Magical Cat**
>
> I am the Magical Cat!
> I don't . . .

Choose one of the brainstorm list. Say 'eat . . .' then make a list all of the things cats usually eat, and pick a couple of these, ideally including some alliterative words:

> I don't eat chicken or tuna

Now list synonyms for 'eat' (some expressive verbs) – and pair together alliterative or rhyming words: gobble/gulp, chomp/chew, munch/crunch . . . Now brainstorm what a magical cat might eat –

> Minty moons, magic stars, lemons, chocolate . . .

Now put these ideas together:

> I am the Magical Cat!
>   I don't eat chicken or tuna
>   I chomp and I chew and I munch and I crunch (for my lunch)
>   minty moons, Magic Stars, Starbursts and a king-size Mars

The poem can be developed further – using more alliteration, and some similes and a song title:

I don't waste my time
    sleeping on walls –
        I race around the universe
            dashing and darting
                from planet to planet

I don't meow or purr – NO!
    I tick like a clock
        I chatter like a chimp
        I whistle like the wind
            et je parle le Français!! (and I speak French!)

And once in a while
    I fly to the roof
        and sing –
            'Reach for the Stars . . .'

This poem was written using 'The Magical Cat' template:

The Fire Tiger

I am not your average tiger,
I am strong,
        fast
            and full of courage.
I don't hunt wild pigs and buffalo.
                I hunt the embers of the fire.
I don't sleep all day,
           I go to work,
I scoff my food
        and go tenpin bowling all night.
I don't just walk in the jungle,
             I run 1200 miles all 24 hours!
I don't just fight for an hour or so,
            I wrestle and box
                11 days a month!
I am the Fire Tiger!

(Kyle Murray – Year 4, RAF Benson Primary School)

3: When I Went to the Year 3000

This activity is based on the poem 'I Went to the Future' by Matthew Sweeney from the collection *Up On the Roof* (Faber & Faber).

Teacher to read out:

Imagine you are on a school trip to the Science Museum in London. At one point you discover you have lost the rest of your party. You are standing in a large room. There is a strange-looking shed in the corner of the room. On closer inspection, you discover it is an old-fashioned machine that has a small doorway. You go through the doorway and find a chair with a computer in front of it. Sitting down, you see printed on the screen 'Would you like to go to the Year 3000?' Without hesitation you type in 'YES!' The next thing you know, you are waking up, going back out of the doorway. Instead of the room in the Science Museum, you are outside in a street. There is very little you recognise. There are people wearing unusual clothes, and vehicles that float off the ground. Before going back into the time machine to the present day, you walk around in the year 3000 to see what the future is like. Think: How do people live? What do they wear/eat? You walk into a home – what is it like? Do children go to school? What transport is there? In what ways is life better or worse than now?

Teacher now brainstorms some of the ideas brought back by the class from the future. These may include such things as:

Robot pets/flying cars/tablet food/floating buildings/a happiness ball

The free verse poem can begin:

When I went
to the year 3000

Now write down the five senses. See – hear – smell – taste – touch. Use these as a guide into each verse of the poem:

I heard
the whoosh and screech
of a low-flying car

I smelt
the pollution
thick in the air

Or, use emotions to start each line:

I was excited
by everyone learning at home

I was thrilled
to discover robot animals
          caring for humans

From here, children could be given the freedom to explore the structure and themes on their own.

4: A Girl's Head

Using the structure of the poem 'A Girl's Head' by Katherine Gallagher on p. 18, write a poem about what might be the contents of someone's – or something's – head. You could even make this an entirely autobiographical poem and include your own thoughts, dreams, fantasies and memories.

Below are some possible titles – feel free to change the title to something that suits your poem best, once you have finished the poem.

- A boy's head
- A teacher's head/a headteacher's head
- A dog/cat/other domestic animal
- A fox/badger/wolf's head

- An elephant's/a tiger's/a shark's head
- An angel's head
- An alien's head/a robot's head
- A soldier's head
- A footballer's head/a pop singer's head

Autobiographical Writing

Free verse allows children to write in their own voices, to use dialect, and to put their own language directly onto the page. The following workshops relate to the model poems 'Night Car Jouney' on p. 17 and 'Straining' on p. 19.

A Mini-Memory

Read through the poem 'Night Car Journey' on p. 17 a few times. Notice how it is written in the present tense – even though the event takes place in the past. This makes the writing more immediate and atmospheric. Choose a special memory of your own. Rather than writing about the entire memory, pick just a few moments. If it was the time you scored a goal, you could describe the few seconds before or after you scored. Or, if it was a holiday, pick just one small aspect of an event from the holiday. Or, maybe as with this poem, you can remember how it felt to be on a journey to somewhere or other. Write your own free verse poem in the present tense. Try to use some of the senses if you can – sight (what can you see?), feel (and is it warm or cold?), sound (what can you hear?) – and, if relevant, smell and taste. Most of all, tell of the experience as if it were happening to you right now.

Openings

Use one of these openings as a starting point for a free verse poem and see where it takes you:

I remember the day . . .

That was the day
that . . .

That was the year/summer/time/day
that I/we . . .

Or a verse for each year of your life:

When I was one
I . . .

When I was two
I . . .

When I was three
I . . .

Memorable Times

Discuss one of these subjects as a starting point into a free verse poem – learning to swim/first day at school/the funniest or the most annoying thing a sibling, parent or friend has done/the weirdest thing ever/the worst holiday ever/a dream/a best friend.

Talking Photos

Write a free verse poem in which you are looking through an imaginary photo album of your life. You could talk about a different photograph/memory in each stanza.

Timeline

Do a timeline for your life. Try to think of things that happened when you were three months/six months/nine months old, and then each year of your life. Pick just one or two memories and celebrate these in some free verse poems. Try not to cram too much detail in. Brainstorm everything first, and then pick some small aspect of each memory to write about.

Starting Points

So often children write poems independently, using their own ideas to create a poem. This method encourages children to create as a community of writers.

Below is a range of titles and opening lines to poems. These are to be written on the board and for children to copy. From there, the children write just the next two lines to the poem, and then the teacher asks for volunteers to read out just their favourite line or phrase. The teacher can write these lines up on the board, commenting on the language used by each child. When there are ten or so disparate lines on the board, the class can be told to start a new poem, using any of the material on the board that they wish, any of their own ideas, or words or phrases from their peers. They do not have to stick to the original title or first lines, they can begin the poem however they wish. With workshops of this nature, children are not writing solely on their own, but are sharing ideas and, hopefully, inspiring one another.

The only rule is that the poems must not rhyme – but they could become calligrams or shape poems. So that children have a model of free verse, photocopy and enlarge either 'Night Car Journey' or 'Hedgehog Hiding at Harvest on Hills Above Monmouth' or 'Straining' and put it up on display.

Moonlit Midnight

Deep in the forest
    there's
        MAGIC

Moongazing

The moon looks very different

The Old House

As the clock struck
          midnight

The Cave Dwellers

Hush!
    Can you hear
          those little voices?

On the Ocean Floor

Deep in the sand
                    it waits

Or pick one of these as a starter:

I'm sitting
                    on a raft
            or – in a desert
            or – on the ocean floor
            or – in a tree
            or – on a mountain
            or – on a cloud

(For further starting lines/titles see pp. 65 & 69.)

The two poems below are perfect examples of how children can take an initial idea and then make it their own. Both of these were written to the title/opening line: 'Moonlit Midnight': Deep in the forest/there's ƆIϘⱯW.

Twinkling Twilight

The Darkness smothers you,
As your sanity silently slips away,
Leaving you floating in nothingness.

The stars glisten overhead,
As your soul battles with magic,
You drift into a trance,
Following paths you do not know,
You're secluded from the outside world,
As the Darkness is
                    fading
                        fading
                            fading

(Louise Rickwood – Year 4, Freeland Primary School)

Owls

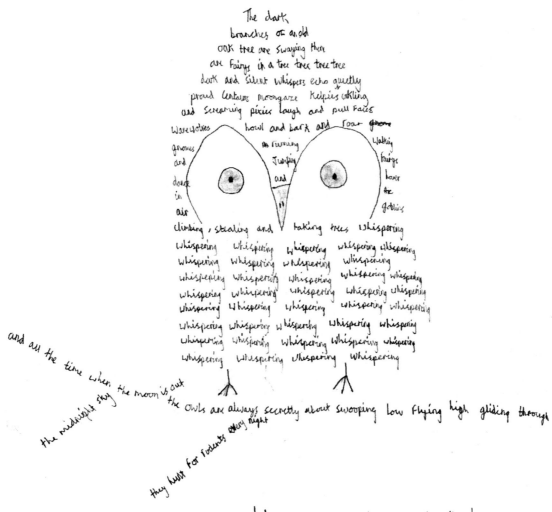

The dark
branches of an old
oak tree are swaying there
are fairys in a tree tree tree tree
dark and silent whispers echo quietly
proud centaurs moongaze Kelpies cackling
and screaming pixies laugh and pull faces
werewolves howl and bark and roar gnome
gnomes Walking
and Fairys
dance hover
in the
air goblins
climbing, stealing and taking trees whispering
whispering whispering whispering whispering whispering
whispering whispering whispering whispering
whispering whispering whispering whispering whispering
whispering whispering whispering whispering whispering
whispering whispering whispering whispering whispering
whispering whispering whispering whispering whispering
whispering whispering whispering whispering whispering
whispering whispering whispering whispering

and all the time when the moon is out
the midnight sky the owls are always secretly about swooping low flying high gliding through
they hunt for rodents every night

but you never see them when its light!

by Francesca Southon

(Francesca Southon, Year 3 – Dorchester St Birinus Primary School)

3

Rhythm and Rhyme

The first word that many people – children and adults – associate with poetry is 'rhyme'. Yet a great number of poems – from free verse to kennings to syllabic verse forms – do not rhyme at all.

For children to become confident and competent writers in rhythm and rhyme, they need to practise their rhyming and rhythmical skills in and out of the context of poetry. This section concentrates on this area, and provides a range of workshops.

Rhythm

Rhythm can be a difficult element of poetry for children to grasp – not so much when reading or performing poetry, but particularly when writing poems. Rhythm is a word that we use most of all when talking about music, and it is just as relevant to poetry. But what is the rhythm of a poem? The rhythm of a poem depends on a number of things, including:

- the words of the poem
- the sounds of the words
- the combination of words used
- the number of syllables in each word/line
- whether there are long vowel sounds (e.g. 'shout') or short vowel sounds (e.g. 'stop')
- whether the poem rhymes or not
- whether there is alliteration or assonance or consonance
- whether there is repetition

but young writers need not be constantly aware of all of these elements as they are writing or reading a poem. One simple way of thinking about rhythm is that it is the flow and feel of the words and the lines of a poem.

One basic rule of rhythm is that you shouldn't just include words to help the rhythm flow. Every word must earn its place in a poem. If it doesn't, it must go! Children need to hear poetry as often as possible so that they can learn to appreciate the cadences, the music and the rhythms of poetic language.

Here are a number of activities in which children can focus on rhythm in order that they can appreciate how it works in poetry:

- *Read* a selection of rhyming poems from this book, such as 'World of Weird' (p. 100), 'Red Boots On' (p. 110), 'Fuss Fuss Fuss' (p. 106), 'The Visitor' (p. 50) and 'Anansi Meets Big Snake'. For the first couple of times read them quietly, and then start to read them out loud. Read slowly and feel the rhythm of each poem.
- *Listen to and read along* with the poems 'Fuss Fuss Fuss', 'World of Weird' and 'Places in

the World' on the CD and concentrate on the rhythm of these poems. Tap your fingers or feet as you listen.

- *Choose* one poem from this book, say 'Fuss Fuss Fuss'. Clap a slow, simple beat 1–2–3–4 to yourself. Say the first two lines of the poem around and around until you have the rhythm tightly fixed in your mind, and then continue clapping as you read the rest of the poem. You will find that the beats fall at these points:

  CLAPS: 1   2   3   4
  Hey, everybody, listen, yo!

  CLAPS: 1   2   3   4
  Here's a tale you might just know

When writing a rhyming poem you will need to keep the rhythm constant throughout the poem. Say the first two, three or even four lines you have written a few times over so that you know the rhythm well. This should help you to keep the rhythm steady throughout the poem. Then try to keep those first few lines at the back of your mind as you are writing your next lines, so that the rhythm is the same. As you begin your poem, if you can't clap or tap your feet out loud, find a rhythm – a constant beat – in your mind's ear.

- Counting *syllables* is a good way to tighten up the rhythm of a poem. As a quick exercise, work out how many many syllables there are in your name. The name of this book – *Page to Stage* – has three. The name of this section – 'Rhythm and Rhyme' has four. On your fingers count the number of syllables there are in some of the rhyming poems in this book, for example – 'World of Weird', 'Fuss Fuss Fuss' and 'Places in the World'. You will find that each line in a rhyming poem has approximately the same number of syllables.

  Hey everybody! Listen, yo! – (eight syllables)
  Here's a tale you might just know (seven syllables)

You should be able to hear if the rhythm of your poem is working as you read it to yourself. If you are ever in any doubt, ask a friend to read the poem out loud to you, and then you will hear if the rhythm is working well.

Rhyme

Even though most poems that children write in the primary years are rhyming poems, these are the most challenging to write really well. To write rhyming poetry young writers need to have a sound appreciation of poetic rhythm as well as a wide vocabulary to produce end-of-line rhymes as well as the patience to rework lines so that the rhythms and rhymes are working well.

As the poet Valerie Bloom says:

Rhyme must be used well. Rhyme, like fire, makes a good servant but a terrible master. You have to stay in control of it. I recommend you don't just use the first word that springs to mind, that you brainstorm alternative words.

The poet Jan Dean also has very useful advice regarding rhyme:

If you start using rhyme at the beginning of a poem, you must use it for the whole piece. But it's perfectly reasonable to have a non-rhyming poem that ends with rhyme, and it can finish a poem off quite nicely. And that can give a poem a bit of extra colour and extra music at the end. I really like using internal rhymes and playing around with rhymes, and putting them in irregular places.

Alongside rhythm, rhyme is what helps to provide the music of a rhyming poem. Two other elements – assonance and alliteration – also play very important roles, but first we will look at rhyme.

What is rhyme? Put simply, rhyming words are those that fall at the end of a line in a poem and have the same sound:

> One too lumpy, one too *hot*
> One just right, she scoffed the *lot*

How often do teachers come across potentially excellent poems by children marred by rhymes which make no sense in the poem? The fundamental rule with rhyme is that not any old word can be used just because it rhymes: if a word doesn't make perfect sense in the poem, it doesn't belong!

There are a number of types of rhyme, and it is perfectly acceptable to use all of these in rhyming poetry.

- *Full rhyme*
  dog/log
  night/bright
- *Half-rhyme* (also known as near-rhyme)
  Sit/pin
  Cat/lap
  Dog/snug
  Cold/had

Half-rhymes such as 'Sit'/'pin' and 'cat'/'lap' use assonance (vowel sounds) and 'dog'/'snug' and 'cold'/'had' use consonance (consonant sounds).

It is better to use a half-rhyme that makes perfect sense in a poem than a word that rhymes well but makes no sense at all. These lines have half-rhymes:

> then I'll pop down to the *shops*
> to stock up on some bits and *bobs*
>
> (from 'Scoff the Sky' by James Carter)

and

> Do I love you
> to the moon and *back*?
> No I love you
> more than *that*
>
> (from 'Love You More' by James Carter)

Find some half-rhymes for these words: tree, new, buy, sink, white, know, near, now, shine, deep, pond.

- *Eye-rhyme* (not so common nowadays)
  rough/through
  show/now
- *Internal rhymes* – where there are rhymes within the lines

  > Hop on a *bee*, pop over the *sea*

Rhymes depend not only on the sounds of the words, but also on the number of syllables:

One syllable: boy/toy, coast/ghost, build/drilled
Two syllable: heaven/seven, bigger/digger, drying/frying
Three syllable: perfecting/reflecting, history/mystery, December/remember

Of these, the single and double syllable rhyming words are more common.

There are different ways of using rhyme in poems. These are called *rhyme schemes*. Have a look at the rhymes in this verse from the poem 'The Walrus and the Carpenter' by Lewis Carroll:

The sun was shining on the sea (A)
    Shining with all his might (B)
He did his very best to make (C)
    The billows smooth and bright – (B)
And this was odd because it was (D)
    The middle of the night. (B)

The rhyme scheme is ABCBDB.

Work out the rhyme scheme for the poem 'A-Sitting on a Gate', also by Lewis Carroll on p. 41.

The poem 'World of Weird' has an ABCDC rhyme scheme:

In the world of Weird
all the oranges are blue
and the lemons are as sweet as can be
bananas are round, and grow in the ground
or down at the bottom of the sea

as well as an *internal rhyme* in every fourth line – here it is 'round' and 'ground'. Read the poem in full on p. 100 to see the other internal rhymes.

When rhymes come at the end of every two lines as in the poem below, the lines are known as *rhyming couplets*:

Now G was out in the woods one day
When after a while she lost her way

Alliteration and *assonance* are closely related to rhyme and are used in all forms of poetry.

Assonance is when words contain the same sounds, but during a line, for example:

'How *far* to the *car*?'

'Is this *my tie*?'

As with rhymes, assonant words have similar sounds but can have very different spellings:

'Where did that *crow go*?'

'I need *four more*.'

General Tips on Rhyming

- Work hard on finding good rhymes. Try not to give up too easily. As Roger McGough says:

  > Usually the best rhyme isn't the first one that pops into your head because that's usually a rather obvious one. Listening to the poem can make ideas for rhymes come because rhymes are part of the music of what you are writing.

- Go through the *alphabet* looking for rhymes. For example, if the word at the end of your last line is 'hat', either in your head or on paper you could go through the ALPHABET putting each letter in front of 'at' to find a suitable rhyme. With the first six letters of the alphabet you would end up with the following – 'aat', 'bat', 'cat', 'dat', 'eat', 'fat' and so on.

- Note that rhymes may sound similar but may look different – such as 'grew'/'shoe' or 'high'/'sky' – and may have a different number of syllables, as in these lines:

  > and the fussiest girl you ever did *see*
  > cooked porridge ever after (quite *happily*)

  (from 'Fuss Fuss Fuss' by James Carter)

- Try not to use a word just because it rhymes. If it doesn't make sense in your poem, then it doesn't belong!

- Go back to your *previous line* and think of different ways of finishing that line, with either a different word or a different phrase that will make it easier for you to find a rhyme in the next line. Or you may find that you need to change the whole of the previous line. Make a list of all the words/phrases you come up with. You could use a thesaurus to help you find alternatives.

- Use a *half-rhyme*. So for 'sit' you may choose 'pin', for 'cat' you may use 'lap' or for 'dog' you may choose 'snug' and for 'cold' you may choose 'had'. 'Sit'/'pin' and 'cat'/'lap' use assonance (vowel sounds) and 'dog' and 'snug' and 'cold' and 'had' use consonance (consonant sounds).

- Use a *rhyming dictionary* if it helps, or ask a friend to help find a rhyme!

Assonance Activity

Note how in this sentence there are many words that sound the same but are spelt differently:

Sue too knew who threw the new shoe in the zoo.

Write your own fun sentences with the words below and using as much assonance as you can. Don't worry if your sentences don't quite make sense!

Found/view/way/bright/sing/moon

Alliteration is when words begin with the same sounds:

'We wish.'

'Short, sharp, shock.'

'Try talking to Tom.'

Look for alliteration in these lines:

watching the clouds

twist and twirl

and

In the world of Weird

all the hamsters hum

Alliteration Activity

This example is quite a tongue twister –

Brainy Brenda brought brilliant Brian some broken brown bricks.

Write your own fun sentences using as much alliteration as you can with some of the words below. Not all of the words that you use have to have the same beginning sound, for example, 'On Tuesday Tim took *his* time.' And don't worry if your sentences don't quite make sense!

Red/cold/five/bubble/grass/lid/creep/many

Anansi Meets Big Snake

Anansi woke with a spidery yawn
and left his hole, to greet the dawn.

But waiting for him, just outside,
was a snake whose jaws lay open wide.

The snake just smiled and gave a hiss,
'Spider for breakfast . . . scrunchy – bliss!'

Anansi didn't gasp or blink.
There wasn't even time to think.

'Oh snake,' he warned, 'I have to say
a snake came by here yesterday.

'And he was big and mean and long,
with ripply muscles, really strong.

'He said that he was saving me
to eat this afternoon, for tea.

'So eat me up and you're a thief
and I guess that snake will give you grief.'

'Another snake as big as me?'
said Snake. 'Round here? Let me see!'

Anansi peered, 'You might be bigger . . .
I'd have to measure up your figure.'

And from the garden by his hole
Anansi picked a bamboo pole.

'Just stretch yourself from end to end.
I need you straight. Try not to bend.

'I'll tie your head here with this vine,
and now your tail. Good, that's fine.

'And now, to get your length just right,
I'll tie your middle nice and tight.'

Anansi scuttled back to take
a look at that enormous snake.

'Oh yes,' he breathed. 'Gigantic. Phew!
I know no snake as big as you.

'The other snake was just a trick
to get you safely on that stick.

'But though you're big, you're not too shrewd.
I must be off now. See ya, dude!'

And so he scuttled on his way
to find some other games to play.

Tony Mitton

Two Limericks

There was a young lady whose chin,
Resembled the point of a pin;
So she had it made sharp,
And purchased a harp
And played several tunes with her chin.

There was an old man of Dumbree,
Who taught little owls to drink tea;
For he said, 'To eat mice,
is not proper or nice,'
That amiable man of Dumbree.

Edward Lear

From
'The Walrus and the Carpenter'

The sun was shining on the sea
    Shining with all his might
He did his very best to make
    The billows smooth and bright
And this was odd because it was
    The middle of the night.

Lewis Carroll

FROM 'A-SITTING ON A GATE'

I'll tell thee everything I can;
    There's little to relate.
I saw an aged aged man,
    A-sitting on a gate.
'Who are you aged man?' I said.
    'And how is it you live?'
And his answer trickled through my head
    Like water through a sieve.

Lewis Carroll

Rhythm and Rhyme Workshops

Practice Poems

Children can write their own verses to the poem 'Down Behind the Dustbin' by Michael Rosen (taken from *You Tell Me* – Puffin) as with these two examples:

> Down behind the dustbin
> I met a dog called Jane
> I said: 'Can I have your number?
> I'd like to meet again.'
>
> (Lucinda Kenrick at Ewelme (C of E) Primary School)

> Down behind the dustbin
> I met a cat called Murray
> he didn't stop to sit and chat
> he dashed off in a hurry
>
> (James Carter)

'Sorry Sorry Sorry' below also acts as a practice model for rhythm and rhyme. It doesn't matter if the verses don't quite make sense, as the emphasis is more on rhythm and rhyme. Write some verses with half-rhymes, if you wish.

Sorry Sorry Sorry

Sorry, I wasn't listening
to a single word you said
I drifted off into the mist
that grew inside my head

Sorry, I wasn't listening
I didn't hear a sound:
I went where dreams of dreams have dreams
and sky and ground swop round

Sorry, I wasn't listening
aliens were at the door
asking for directions to
the planet XR4

Sorry, I wasn't listening
some pirates came for me
first I had to walk the plank
and then I made them tea

Sorry, I wasn't listening
I don't know what went on
could you say it one more time –
hang on – where've you gone?

(James Carter)

Anansi Poems

Tony Mitton's poem 'Anansi Meets Big Snake' tells of a popular figure in African and Afro-Carribean folklore, Anansi the spider-man. Note how the poem is written in rhyming couplets. Note too that each line has between seven and ten syllables.

The final line of Tony Mitton's poem says that Anansi went off 'to find some other games to play'. What games could they be? What other animals or people could he trick? Make a list of some animals, and think of how Anansi could trick them.

Here are some possible opening lines for a new poem:

> Now next, Anansi bumped into
> a creature from the local zoo . . .

> One afternoon in late July
> Anansi bumped into a fly
> Anansi said: ' . . .

Limericks

Read through the two limericks by Edward Lear on p. 40 Listen to the rhythm and pay attention to the rhyme schemes: AABBA. Now write a few limericks of your own.

Nonsense Poems 1

Write some verses using this list poem structure:

> My name is beware-of-the-dog
> My name is free-inside
> My name is kittens-for-sale
> My name is park-and-ride

> (after Pauline Clarke)

You can vary the rhyme scheme from ABCB (as above) to rhyming couplets – AABB.

Nonsense Poems 2

Read 'World of Weird' on p. 100. Note the ABCDC rhyme scheme, and how the fourth line has an internal rhyme. Now write a verse or two of your own.

Nonsense Poems 3

Read Lewis Carroll's 'Jabberwocky' on p. 118. Read the poem through a number of times. Get to know the rhythm of the poem well. Feel comfortable with the pronunciations of the words. Now write your own verses using your own invented words. This poem has an ABAB rhyme structure, but you can vary this. In your poem you could:

- turn words around, for example: petcar (carpet) lingcei (ceiling)
- mix words and numbers: tenboy or twocat
- mix beginnings of words: goys and birls or dats and cogs
- simply invent your own words!

If you want a starter for your poem, you could adapt the opening line to 'Jabberwocky'. The word 'brillig' means evening, so, your opening line could take the word 'morning' and make the anagram 'ningmor':

> 'Twas ningmor and the . . . . . .

Raps 1 – Narrative Raps

Read through the fairy tale rap in this book, 'Fuss Fuss Fuss' (p. 106) a few times. See how the rap tells a story. Find another fairy tale ('Three Little Pigs', 'Snow White', 'Cinderella', 'Jack and the Beanstalk' or 'Sleeping Beauty') or novel (a *Harry Potter* book, a Jacqueline Wilson book such as *Tracy Beaker* or an Anthony Horowitz book) or a Disney film (*Toy Story, Finding Nemo*) and adapt the story into a rap poem.

Tips on writing raps:

- Read through the 'Rhythm and Rhyme' section of this book for tips on using rhythm and rhyme.
- Brainstorm some ideas first – for instance, write down character names, details from the story, find any rhyming words (e.g. 'sticks' and 'bricks' or 'pigs' and 'digs' from 'Three Little Pigs' or 'Cinderella' and 'fella').
- Keep the rhythm as tight as you can – write your rap to a slow and steady beat – clap along as you write (if you are struggling, keep re-reading the rap in this book and listen to the rhythms).
- Chant your first few lines over a few times in your head to make sure you know the rhythm of your rap well.
- You will need to do a few drafts of your rap poem. In the first draft, don't worry too much about the rhythm or the rhymes, concentrate on getting down all the ideas that come to you. In your second or third draft you can improve the poem by working on the rhythm and the rhymes and the overall flow of the rap.
- Use modern language – such as 'yo', 'cool', 'dude', 'bling', 'keep it real' and 'da hood'.
- Shorten the names – Harry Potter could be 'HP', Cinderella could be 'Little Miss C', Hansel and Gretel could be 'H&G' or the 'Three Little Pigs' could be the 'Three Little Ps'.
- Use half-rhymes – and try not to include any old word simply because it rhymes!
- Add a chorus for your audience to join in on – see the simple three-word chorus in the rap 'Fuss Fuss Fuss' which is 'Fiss, Fuss, Fuss', or for a rap of 'The Three Little Pigs' you could have a chorus along the lines of:

    I'll huff and I'll puff and I'll blow you down
    I'll blow you guys right out of town!

    Why not pick a fairy tale that already has a chant or rhyme and build a rap around it? 'Jack and the Beanstalk' has 'Fe fi fo fum'; 'Snow White' has 'Mirror, mirror on the wall'.
- Check those syllables (keep to more than seven and fewer than eleven syllables per line).
- Don't re-tell the whole story – start half-way through if you wish.
- Change the ending of the story – note the ending to 'Fuss Fuss Fuss'.
- Have fun by changing the point of view to a story. Most fairy tales are written in the third person – 'Once upon a time there lived . . .' So write a rap in the first person, from one character's point of view – for instance 'Little Red Riding Hood' in the wolf's voice or 'Cinderella' in one of the sister's voices.

Or, take a story you have written (or want to write) and tell it in the form of a rap. You can use one of these introductions:

Once, in a land far far way . . .

Once there lived . . .

This is the tale/story/rap of . . .

Hey, everybody! Listen – yo
here's a tale you might just know . . .

Have a look at Roald Dahl's hilarious *Revolting Rhymes* – these are very close to fairy tale raps. Two modern poets who write rap poems are Tony Mitton and Benjamin Zephaniah – have a look at their work for some great examples of rap poetry.

Raps 2 – Autobiographical Raps

Read through the rap 'Fuss Fuss Fuss' a few times. Now write a rap poem about your own experiences or your life or your world view. Use modern language – your own language or dialect. If you speak a number of languages, why not include words and phrases in each language? You could include a memory from each year of your life. Here are some opening lines:

> Brothas and sistas in da hood
> listen hard and listen good
> My name is . . .
>
> Hey everybody, listen to me
> check this out from your MC
> My name is . . .

You could also rap about your friends, your school, the place where you live, your hobbies (music, football, fashion, etc.) – anything that interests you. Have a listen to a range of rap artists from Eminem to Dizzee Rascal and see how they play with rhythm and rhyme and weave magic with words.

Raps 3 – Keep it Real Raps

Write a rap with a message – on topics such as the environment, recycling, bullying, respect for all cultures, homelessness, endangered species, violence, caring for people – or anything that interests and concerns you.

Raps 4 – School/Class Raps

This workshop can be done by individuals or small groups or as a whole class with the teacher scribing. First, decide if you want to write about the class or the school as a whole. A class rap could be performed in a class assembly, and a school rap could be written to coincide with a special event for the school.

Then brainstorm ideas. What do you want to rap about? One verse could be introducing the teacher(s), another verse certain children, and other verses could cover special events at the school, recent concerts/plays/sports matches or the history of the school/local area.

Here is a possible opening:

> Everybody in the school/class, listen, yo!
> Here's some stuff you'll need to know

If you are writing for performance, it is good to have a chorus in the rap – something that the audience or whole class/school can learn and join in with.

4

Image and Metaphor

The poet Matthew Sweeney quotes Robert Frost when he says: 'Poetry is a fresh look and a fresh listen.' This serves as a very useful approach. It encourages us to aim for something new and 'fresh' when creating a poem, not only in terms of *what* we are writing about, for example a new way of thinking about a subject, but also 'fresh' in terms of *how* the poem is expressed – in terms of the language and the imagery that we use. The poet Colin Macfarlane says very much the same thing when he states that in poetry 'a good description gives a new way of seeing'.

This section may seem to deal with two unconnected areas – imagery and metaphor – but really the two are very much connected, as ultimately, metaphors (as well as similes) and imagery are both concerned with giving the reader pictures in the mind's eye.

Read through Helen Dunmore's poem 'Hedgehog Hiding' on p. 40. Notice how visual the poem is, and what unusual but very effective words – including metaphors – she uses to describe the grass:

> moon-stripped grass ripples like tiger skin

and the ditch:

> the dry ditch rustles with crickets

and also how the poet shows that the hedgehog is still and quiet:

> in your ball of silence
> your snorts muffled
> your squeaks and scuffles
> gone dumb

When writing visually one must remember to *show* and not to *tell*. 'Telling' is saying something like 'the house was scary' or 'the sunset was beautiful' – and is lazy, ineffective writing that communicates very little. Poems need to be specific and to give detail. 'Flamingo pink, the burning sun dipped beneath the rippling sea' in just a few words gives the reader a great deal of information and *shows why* the sunset was beautiful. Likewise, 'the house was riddled with rot and dust, and late at night it creaked and moaned itself to sleep' begins to give a full picture and is *showing why* the house is scary. Other words used that give little effect are 'nice' and 'spooky' – and are best avoided!

The fiction writer Morris Gleitzman suggests, 'Let your readers see, hear, smell, taste and touch your story' – the same is just as true with poetry. Even close your eyes occasionally and imagine the setting or the subject of your poem in your mind's eye as vividly as you can. As Valerie Bloom advises, 'You need to explore the image and not be happy with the first descriptive word or phrase you come across.' You can also use a thesaurus to help you find a choice of words and phrases.

Try writing a short piece or poem about a house. Use the five senses to bring the house to life in your writing. So not only should you describe what it looks like, but what does the room smell of? Is there a variety of smells? What sounds are in the room – a clock ticking, a creaking floorboard – or is it totally silent? Are there noises outside – a road drill or a train rushing past? Is the room warm or cold – and is it warmer by the window where the sun comes in? What are the textures of various items in the room – the carpet, the chair, the cushions, and so on.

It is also worth paying attention to verbs and adverbs. It is far better to use a strong, expressive verb than a weak verb that has to rely on an adverb to qualify it. 'The old man walked slowly down the lane' is not as effective as 'The old man hobbled down the lane.' In a first draft of any piece of writing it is easy to over-write and include too many adjectives and adverbs. Therefore it is worth checking in a second or third draft for such areas as adjectives – too many and the effect is lost. 'The little, angry, fluffy, yappy white dog' is not as powerful as 'the little yappy dog'. Less is always more.

What is a metaphor? Metaphoric language (otherwise known as 'figurative' language) compares one thing to another. The old cliché 'It's raining cats and dogs' is a metaphor – because it says that the rain *is* made of cats and dogs. But to state that 'the rain is as hard as nails' would be a simile, because it says that the rain is not actually, but like nails. A simile will always use the words 'as' or 'like' to compare one thing to another. In Helen Dumore's poem there is one simile and a number of metaphors. See if you can spot them.

Again, when using metaphors it is important to *be original* and *avoid clichés*. A cliché is an unoriginal or overused phrase or description. Here is an example of a cliché –

> The lovely sky
> is full of cotton wool clouds . . .

Instead, you could try something like:

> A gang of scruffy clouds
> shuffle across an ice-blue sky

This phrase has an unusual but powerful metaphor – that of a 'gang' of clouds 'shuffling'. And the second part of the sentence gives the reader a vivid description of the sky with just two simple words – 'ice-blue'.

Haiku poems are perfect for capturing an image as well as a single moment in space and time. Haikus have been described as little 'snapshots'. This three-verse haiku has three separate images all building up to a whole picture:

> On a frozen pond
> a small dog is nervously
> attempting to skate

> Way up in the tree
> a black cat grins with delight
> watching and waiting

> Beneath the clear ice
> a big fish wonders if all
> dogs walk on water

> ('Icy Morning Haiku' by James Carter)

Another useful quote from Matthew Sweeney is 'The big enemy in poetry is vagueness, the other cliché' – which encourages young writers to be adventurous and imaginative and to take risks in the language and the imagery they use in their writing.

Hedgehog Hiding at Harvest in the Hills Above Monmouth

Where you hide
    moon-stripped grass ripples like tiger skin
where you hide
    the dry ditch rustles with crickets

where you hide
    the electricity pylon saws and sighs
and the combine harvester's headlight
pierces the hedges

where you hide
    in your ball of silence
    your snorts muffled
    your squeaks and scuffles
    gone dumb

a foggy moon sails over your head,
the stars are nipped in the bud

where you hide
    you hear the white-faced owl hunting
    you count the teeth of the fox

Helen Dunmore

The Visitor

Cold fingers clawed the face of earth,
Bold winter strutted round,
Bare branches trembled in the wind,
Their leaves mulching the ground.
Dancing snowflakes chuckled in the
Prancing north-east breeze,
Algid river stood still, crippled,
Aged women coughed and wheezed.
Sheep shivered in the snow-bound wasteland,
Steep and icy were the paths.
In the houses, people huddled,
Skin slowly cooking round the hearths.
Then it happened, one clear morning,
When the bite of cold was sore,
That there came a gentle knocking
At the weatherman's cottage door.
He got out and shambled out to
See, his heart began to sing,
By the door, a young girl smiling,
'Hi,' she said. 'My name is Spring.'

Valerie Bloom

Grandma

Grandma is navy blue.
She is a comfy cushion.
Grandma is a soft whisper.
She is a path through a winter wood.
Grandma is a warm scarf.
She is a cup of tea by the fire.
Grandma is a sleeping cat.
She is autumn sunshine.

John Foster

Image and Metaphor Workshops

Animal Similies

Take an animal and build up an image stage by stage in a short poem.

Shark

Skin as smooth as still water
eyes that shine like deep black pearls
a fin as pointed as an evil mountain
teeth as sharp as jagged glass

(James Carter)

Choose an animal first, and then brainstorm some of its features. If you choose an owl you could list: eyes, feathers, claws and beak. Then search for some unusual and original similes to describe your animal with. Note how, in the poem above, there are adjectives in the similes, which make the image stronger – '*deep black* pearls', '*jagged* glass' '*still* water' and '*evil* mountain'.

'At Night'

A list-poem of images. Teacher-led activity: children first brainstorm anything to do with night-time – such as darkness, shadows, sleep, silence, stars, the moon, bats, moths, foxes, cats and so on. The teacher can model some lines and encourage the class to think of effective verbs and similes to describe events at night.

At Night

At night the darkness spreads
over the world like a soft blanket
the shadows creep like ghosts
the bats shriek so so loud
and the stars twinkle so so bright

At night hedgehogs are scurrying
through the leaves
foxes are looking for food
the owls are hooting really loud
bats are flying round the trees

At night the howling wind rattles the windows
it is so dark and windy that the branches
look like fierce claws
the thunder is roaring like a raging lion

(Jessie Duckworth, Year 2, Broadlands Primary School, Hereford – from a workshop with poet Peter Cutts)

Draw with Words

The verse below is inspired by John Foster's poem 'I'm Painting a Picture' (from *You Little Monkey!* – Oxford University Press) in which in each verse the narrator paints a picture of a different subject.

I'm drawing a picture of an elf
with rosy cheeks
and pointy ears
scurrying barefoot
through the snow.

Now write your own verses, each beginning 'I'm drawing a picture of a/an . . .' Like John Foster, you could choose a dragon, wizard, ghost or giant or something else – say a dolphin, an alien or a dinosaur. Make sure your reader can really see the creature you are writing about: in this poem we know the elf has rosy cheeks, pointy ears and has no shoes. And there is one very colourful verb: 'scurrying'. Let your reader see your creature through your words.

'Grandma'/Metaphoric People

Read the poem 'Grandma' by John Foster on p. 51 a few times. Using the same structure, write about someone you know, so:

- . . . is a (colour)
- . . . is a (piece of furniture)
- . . . is a (sound)
- . . . is a (landscape)
- . . . is a (piece of clothing)
- . . . is a (food or drink)
- . . . is a (animal)
- . . . is a (form of weather)

Feel free to change the order and add your own metaphors. Try to pick the best and most suitable metaphors you can.

Haikus

Read some of the haiku poems in this book on p. 47 and p. 80. Note how these are all made up of three lines, and have a syllable count of 5 (first line)/7 (second line)/5 (third line). Write your own haiku:

- *Animal*: write a haiku about an animal in a single moment – such as: a dolphin the moment it leaps above a wave/the moment a bird catches its prey/a dog asleep.
- *Utopia/dystopia*: write a two-verse haiku: one describing your perfect world, and the other your least perfect world. These can be funny – if you want them to be!

Kennings

Kennings are ancient poems that originally came from Scandinavia. Each two-word line brings together two different things (as in 'swamp-swimmer' and 'jaw-snapper' below) to create a metaphor, and ultimately, a full image of its subject, often an animal. Having two words in each line sets up a rolling rhythm. Kennings are as much fun to perform as they are to write.

Popular topics include pets – cats, dogs, rabbits and so on. You could do one about a friend of yours or a member of your family – or a character from a book or film or TV programme. If you were to pick a cat, brainstorm many things that cats do – lick their fur (so one line could become 'fur-licker'), chase mice ('mouse-chaser'), and so on. Think – what does this animal/person/character love/hate/dream about/long for/need? And though this poem below does occasionally rhyme, it is not necessary to always include any rhymes at all.

What Am I?

I'm a . . .
long-goner
swamp-swimmer
loud-stomper
slow-plodder
meat-muncher
brain-cruncher
heart-breaker
head-banger
jaw-snapper
teeth-gnasher
fierce-fighter
comet-hater
foul-smeller
museum-dweller
What am I? . . . a dinosaur!

(Year 1 and 2 classes – Dorchester St Birinus Primary School with James Carter)

Human Touch

Valerie Bloom's poem 'The Visitor' (p. 50) is an example of metaphoric language used to great effect. One type of metaphor the poet uses here is personification. See how she gives human characteristics to many different things:

> Bold winter strutted round . . . Dancing snowflakes chuckled . . . By the door, a young girl smiling/'Hi,' she said. 'My name is Spring.'

Instead of going straight into a poem using personification, think of ways to describe the world around you in human terms, such as:

The sky/clouds/rain/snow/the sun
The night sky/stars/the moon/the dark
The sea/the waves/the beach/cliffs
The city/the streets/the traffic/the shops/a river
A forest/the trees/the leaves/the animals

Then pick the one you like the most and develop it into either a rhyming or a free verse poem.

Metaphor and Description

Think of unusual ways to describe the following in the most original way that you can, without going over the top. This does not have to be a poem as such, perhaps a few phrases or a sentence.

- a full or crescent moon
- a starry night
- a sunset
- a storm at sea
- a mountain
- a view of earth from space

- a snow-covered forest
- a snow-capped mountain
- a swimming pool at midnight
- the rain
- an empty house

My Name Is

Write a first-person poem in which you become the subject of the poem – for example, the future, the wind, the moon, the sun, the sky, the sea, a river, a cloud. The poem could be written as a free verse poem. Here is a poem in which the narrator is time:

Talking Time

Not only the day but also the night
I am the coming and going of light

The growing and turning of shadows on land
the falling of sand, that watch on your hand

The arc of the moon, the tug of the tides
the till of the fields, the sun as it hides

The here and the now and the way back when
in hide and seek games: the counting to ten

Your birthday, your diary, the lines on your face
the start and the finish of every race

Measure me, treasure me, do as you will
I'll drag or I'll fly but I'll never stay still

If I am your rhythm, then you are my rhyme
we live for each other, and my name is time

(James Carter)

New Similes

As the poet Matthew Sweeney says when quoting Robert Frost, 'poetry is a fresh look and listen'. In poetry it is important to avoid clichéd language and to think of new and exciting ways of talking about the world around us. The following short exercise encourages children to think up new similes, and some lines could even be developed into stanzas of a poem.

As cold as . . . (not ice!)

As hot as . . .

As big as . . .

As quiet as . . . (not a mouse!)

As loud as . . .

As bright as . . .

As dull as . . .

As dark as . . .

As red as . . .

As green as . . .

As spotty as . . .

As stripy as . . .

As fast as . . . (not a cheetah!)

As slow as . . .

As hungry as . . .

As tired as . . .

As wild as . . .

As tall as . . .

As tiny as . . .

'The Visitor'

Read the poem 'The Visitor' by Valerie Bloom a few times. Think of ways you could write a poem in this style, but on a different season – spring, summer or autumn. Your poem does not have to rhyme though. You could aim for a free verse poem that lists different features of the season, as in this brainstorm:

Autumn

Autumn never stops
so much to do
before the winter

weaving carpets of leaves on the ground
painting sunsets of purples and pinks
bringing children back to school
searching for scarves long packed away . . .

World of Metaphors

The following is a structure for a free verse poem to encourage similes and metaphors and can be used or adapted in any way:

The world is not
what it seems
The sea . . .
    (example – hisses like an angry cat)
The wind is/has . . .
    (example: has a terrible tantrum temper)
The clouds . . .
The trees are . . .
The rain is . . .
The moon is . . .
The sun is . . .

These lines can alternatively be written as similes, e.g. 'the wind is rolling like an angry wildcat'. Alternatively, poems can be an extension of one line, a conceit – an extended metaphor, for example:

> The wind has a terrible tantrum temper
> chucking its toys across the land . . .

Where You Hide

Read the poem 'Hedgehog Hiding at Harvest in Hills Above Monmouth' by Helen Dunmore on p. 49 a few times. Think of another animal that might be hiding somewhere – say a leopard in a tree ready to pounce on its prey, a fox hiding in a wood during a hunt, or a cat stuck outside in a bush on a rainy day waiting for its owner to return home. Do a brainstorm. Think: what does the animal look like? Why is it hiding? Where is it hiding? What would it be thinking about? Keep returning to Helen Dunmore's poem and think of imaginative and descriptive ways of describing the animal, its location and its situation. Once you have brainstormed enough thoughts, write a free verse poem, perhaps using the phrase 'Where you hide' to begin each verse. Be adventurous and imaginative with your language, metaphors and descriptions.

5

A Range of Poetry Writing Workshops

This section features a wide variety of poetry writing workshops which can be adapted according to class ability levels, interests and needs.

Abstractions

This poetry has been popularised by the poets Carol Ann Duffy and Matthew Sweeney. Think of some abstract nouns, some that you have experienced yourself – such as happiness, jealousy, excitement, confusion, greed, boredom, disappointment, compassion, tiredness, surprise, love, worry, hate, contentment or hope. Make a list and decide which one interests you most. Think about your abstraction imaginatively and put it into real terms by answering the following questions, which have been answered for the abstraction 'confusion':

1. What does it look like? *Grey as an afternoon that never quite rains.*
2. What does it sound like? *Musak in a shopping centre.*
3. What does it taste like? *White bread – no butter or jam.*
4. What does it feel like? *So itchy you want to scratch it all the time.*
5. Where does it live? *In a cupboard and falls out every time you open it.*
6. What does it smell like? *School dinners.*
7. What would it say if it could speak? *Anything – but it would go on and on and on!*

Bring your own responses together and draw them together into a free verse poem. Each separate answer could be expanded into a whole stanza.

Call and Response Chant Poems

'Deep in the Forest' (this is a variation of the poetry workshop on p. 29): children are given the line 'Deep in the forest', which in performance will be whispered by the whole class, and the second lines will be spoken by one child. Children write their own call and response poems to 'Deep in the forest' – for example:

Deep in the forest/at night-time
Deep in the forest/there's magic
Deep in the forest/up in the trees
Deep in the forest/and all around
Deep in the forest/it's mischief time
Deep in the forest/elves are prancing
Deep in the forest/wolves are hollering . . .

As with this example, the poem does not have to rhyme. Try and keep to no more than four or five syllables per response line. This poem can be written by individuals or small groups or even as a whole class with the teacher as scribe. The latter will give it a more communal feel right from the start.

The line 'Deep in the forest' could be changed after a number of lines to something like 'Under the stone' or 'High in a tree' or 'Deep in a cave' – and these could be repeated for a certain number of times.

'Late at Night' – children are given the line 'Late at night'. This will be whispered by the whole class, and one child will respond with the next lines. Children write their own responses to 'Late at night' – for example:

> Late at night – when no one's about
> Late at night – when all is still
> Late at night – in a dark dark town
> Late at night – in a lonely street
> Late at night – go through the gate
> Late at night – walk up the path
> Late at night – now open the door
> Late at night – to the empty house
> Late at night – and walk right in . . .

Further call and response lines:

> In the house on the hill – . . .
> In the rainforest – . . .
> In the desert – . . .
> Out in space – . . .
> Under the sand – . . .
> Deep in the cave – . . .

The Five Senses

Morris Gleitzman says that young writers need to 'Let your readers see, hear, smell, taste and touch your story.' And this applies to poetry too.

Using the five senses can bring your poems to life. Read through this extract of a class poem written by Willow Class (Year 3) at Wolston St Margaret's C of E Primary School:

Harvest Senses

> Listen listen, what do you hear?
> the rumbling of the tractor
> cutting down the golden corn
> cheeping birds flapping their wings
> rustling leaves falling to the ground
>
> (Ssh! Ssh! Ssh!)
>
> Look, look, what do you see?
> Busy workers harvest crops from the field,
> I glance at the tall yellow corn, waving at me,
> See the bright, shining apples, stacked in a basket,
> Tractor wheels busily rolling along.

(Look! Look! Look!) (pointing)

Taste, taste, what can I eat?
savoury buttery new potatoes, boiling in the pot
tasty red and green peppers, so spicy to eat
try those reeking onions, bringing tears to your eyes
nibble a crunchy yellow pear
lovely and fresh from the tree

(Yum! Yum! Yum!)

Sniff, sniff, what can I smell?
juicy peaches dangling from the tree,
rotten tomatoes falling squashy and round,
fresh orange carrots, plucked from the field,
can I smell those sweet rosy red apples?
the scent of juicy strawberries fills the air.
smell those earthy potatoes, freshly dug.

(Sniff . . . sniff . . . sniff . . .)

Feel, feel, what do you touch?
bumpy potatoes from deep underground,
carefully feel that soggy soil, all crumbly and brown,
squishy blackberries hanging from the bush,
lovely and juicy, so soft to touch,
feel the caress of the blowing wind,
the touch of the gently swaying, golden corn.

(Woo! Woo! Woo!)

Harvest has come!

Choose a celebration to write a poem about – birthday, Diwali, bonfire night, Hallowe'en, Christmas or Hanukkah. Use the opening lines from the poem above if you wish – such as 'Listen, listen, what do you hear?' and cover one sense per verse.

Friendship Poem

This workshop – devised by Pie Corbett and Brian Moses – is based on an ancient Chinese ceremony established over 2,000 years ago.

I want to be friends with you
till all the seas have turned to ice
and the moon has drifted away
bored with haunting us

If we are friends –

I will make you
a forever friend
be true to you
and give you
even my

very

last

crisp

If I could I would give you
the tear of an angel
a priceless pearl
and the last drop of light
from the first day of summer

I will like you more than
days on the beach
climbing a hill
or watching a shower
of shooting stars

(James Carter)

Use the same structure to write your own friendship poem:

I want to be friends with you . . .

If we are friends –

I will . . .

If I could I would give you . . .

I will like you more than . . .

Forms of Poetry

There are many books that specialise in detailing the various poetic forms. Covered in this book are: free verse (p. 12), rhyming verse (p. 32), raps (p. 44), haiku (p. 53), acrostic (p. 10), cinquain (p. 80), kennings (p. 53), and shape poems (p. 67). See 'Forms of Poetry' (p. 78) for ideas of forms to experiment with.

Others you may wish to explore, and that are all covered in Sandy Brownjohn's *To Rhyme or Not to Rhyme?* (Hodder) are:

- Ballad
- Clerihew
- Diamond
- Sonnet
- Tanka
- Villanelle

Going Places

Have a read through the song lyric 'Places in the World' (p. 104). Now write a poem in rhyming couplets about travelling around the UK.

Brainstorm:

- One-syllable place names, such as – Brent, Kent, Wells, Slough, Bath, Leeds, Stroud, York.
- Two-syllable place names, such as – St Ives, Reading, Swindon, Sheffield, Warwick, Cardiff, Dublin, Bristol, London, Swansea, Selsey, Cambridge, Swanage, Glasgow.
- Three-syllable place names, such as – Birmingham, Manchester, Dagenham, Liverpool, Coventry, Southampton, etc.

Match together those that rhyme. You can use this two-line introduction and then write your own couplets to follow.

I need a ticket to catch a train
from here to there and back again:

Hartlepool, Dagenham, Redditch and Kent
Liverpool, Birmingham, Reading and Brent

List Poems

A list poem starts each line or verse with the same phrase. 'A Girl's Head' (p. 18), 'Hedgehog Hiding' (p. 49), 'Electric Guitars' (p. 102) 'At Night' (p. 52) and 'Grandma' (p. 51) are all list poems.

Brian Moses: 'Pick one of the phrases below and use it as a starting point for a list poem. Start every line or every stanza with the same word or phrase.'

I wish I was . . .

It's a secret but . . .

I dreamt I . . .

Don't . . .

I'd rather be . . .

I like . . .

If only . . .

Magic Box

The poem 'Magic Box' by Kit Wright is one of the most popular model poems in primary schools today. Note how in the version below, the poet has carefully chosen her words to create some magical imagery and concepts. She has used a lot of alliteration to add music to the poem, and she has created some effective contrasts – 'the first day on earth/the last claw of a dragon' and 'a wolf in the sea and a dish on land'.

The Magic Box
(after Kit Wright)

I will put in the box
a sip of the silky shiny sea,
a delicate dazzling diamond,
the violet velvet voice of a vampire.

I will put in the box
the first day on earth,

the last claw of a dragon.
I will put in the box
a dog in a hutch and a rabbit in a kennel,
a wolf in the sea and a fish on land.

My box is made of gold –
its hinges are made of steel with rubies in it,

My box is as big as my hand
but it can hold the universe.

I will keep my secrets in my box
but sometimes I will say the magic words
and get into my box and look at my secrets.

(by Connie Jacobs, Ewelme (C of E) Primary School)

Write about your own magic box, and what you would choose to include inside it. Think of the most fantastic things you can imagine. Really let your imagination go. Include some of your own powerful alliterative phrases such as 'a delicate dazzling diamond' or 'the violet velvet voice of a vampire'.

See the 'Model Poems' workshop below.

Magic Potions

Read the poem below, which is based on the witches' speech from Shakespeare's *Macbeth*. Note how the young poet has borrowed the first two and last two lines from the original text – on p. 108. Write your own version, with your own gruesome ingredients! Try to inject some alliteration if you can, such as 'slithery snake' or even internal rhymes such as 'trail of snail'.

Witches' Potion

Double, double, toil and trouble;
Fire burn and cauldron bubble.
Eye of dragon, tail of cat,
Heart of frog, wing of bat;
Mouldy spider, rabbit's tail,
Big tomatoes all gone stale.
Heart of rat and old man's beard,
Type of potion – really weird.
For a charm of powerful trouble
Like a hell-broth, boil and bubble.

(by Ellie Clements, Year 4 Ewelme (C of E) Primary School)

Model Poems

Find a poem that you like, and use one of these ideas for writing your own poem:

* Borrow the title and write your own poem to it – and once you have written your own poem, you could even think of a new title if you wish.
* Borrow the opening line and write a poem to it – again, you could put in an opening line

of your own if you wanted to once you have finished – and remember to state at the bottom where you borrowed the line from.

- Write some new stanzas for a poem you like.
- Write a new poem in the same style, using the same voice, tone and language.
- If your poem is narrated by one character, write another poem in that voice.
- If your poem is in a set form – perhaps a rhyming poem, free verse, haiku or kenning – write a new poem in that form.
- Retell a favourite story in the form of a poem – perhaps a fairy tale, fable, myth or legend – and do not worry about including all of the original details.
- Write a poem in the voice of a character from a novel – say Tracy Beaker from Jacqueline Wilson's *The Story of Tracy Beaker/The Dare Game* or the twins from Jacqueline Wilson's *Double Act* or Harry or Hermione from J. K. Rowling's *Harry Potter* books or Michael in Michael Morpurgo's *Kensuke's Kingdom*.

There are numerous model poems provided throughout this book, including the 'Magic Box' workshop above.

Music

Music has been used as a stimulus for creative writing workshops for years. Many contemporary authors and poets use it in their own writing. Instrumental music is most effective, and try film soundtracks which have many sequences of atmospheric music. Teachers could even try the music CD accompanying the teacher's book *Just Imagine* (David Fulton) – by the author of this book! – which has eight instrumental tracks written specifically for poetry and creative writing workshops at KS2, in a range of genres, styles, moods, tones and atmospheres.

Children often need to hear a piece of music at least twice. Some children ask for the music to continue playing softly for the duration of the workshop. Clearly, as with all writing, full concentration is vital, and it may help if the class close their eyes initially. The result will essentially be raw material, a mass of thoughts and notes or a 'stream of consciousness' that will then have to be shaped and developed into a coherent piece of writing.

Children can either improvise a poem (free verse) as they listen, or brainstorm thoughts, images, words, phrases, titles, memories, feelings, emotions, descriptions of people or places or events – everything that comes to them. From there, either the teacher can collect ideas and write a group poem with the class, or individual children could sift through their brainstorm notes searching for material for a poem – a title, an opening line, an image, a narrative or whatever.

Two other useful things to consider when listening to music:

- *the five senses* – what you can see, hear, smell, touch and taste – write down everything that relates to these, things that can be seen, heard and so on.
- general questions such as: *What? Where? When? Why? How?* – so what is happening? – where/when is it taking place? – why is it happening?

Musical Instruments

Read the poem 'Electric Guitars' on p. 102. Now choose a musical instrument and brainstorm all the words you can about the instrument: What it looks like (could you use any similes?). What it sounds like. Listen to all the sounds mentioned in the poem – choppy, angry, chirpy, jangling, twanging, etc. You could even make up your own onomatopoeic words – and your own adjectives and verbs or similes and metaphors to describe these sounds. Also think about what styles of music your instrument plays. What songs might it play? What people might play that instrument? What other instruments might it play alongside? Get a poem together – rhyming or non-rhyming – that uses some of these ideas. Include alliterating words too. Perhaps you could write a non-rhyming poem with a catchy, rhyming chorus. Or you could invent and design an instrument of the future; give the instrument a name, then draw an outline and write a poem inside.

Opening Lines

Pick an opening line and use it for a poem – rhyming or free verse – of your own.

> Once upon a while ago . . .
>
> In the year 3084 . . .
>
> Today's the day
> that pigs will fly . . .
>
> Don was a terrible dragon . . .
>
> That house down the road
> is empty now . . .
>
> All of a sudden . . .

People Poems

Roger Stevens:

> I find writing list poems a very useful exercise. It works well with children of all ages and abilities because it's based on a very simple idea, it introduces very clearly the concept of first, second and third (or more) drafts and it's fun! I first read a list poem, usually 'Socks' by Colin West, which is in *The Works* (Pan Macmillan – compiled by Paul Cookson). I use 'Socks' because it has a great rhythm, a simple introduction and a neat ending. Most importantly, it is a long poem, and demonstrates that even with a simple subject such as socks it is possible to create a long, varied and interesting list and poem.
>
> Next, we brainstorm ideas for lists. Subjects need to be neither too vague nor specific. For example, animals (too vague), dogs (just right), poodles (too specific). Good subjects: hats, shoes, cats, snakes, sharks, chocolate, pizzas, etc.
>
> The poem 'Ten Pin Bowling' by Timothy Hopper came about during a longer character workshop with a Year 5 class. We used the list poems exercise as a warm up and the pupils had to choose types of people for their list – e.g. mums, teachers, sisters, policemen/women, footballers, etc. I then asked each pupil to make a list on their chosen subject. At this stage I stress it is a list and not a poem – and state that the subject word (e.g. dog, shoe, etc.) need not be mentioned every time – so instead of blue hat, green hat, bowler hat, top hat – you could write blue, green, bowler, top. In this brainstorming session I discourage use of the dictionary and ask children not to worry about neatness or spelling.
>
> I give the class four minutes exactly, and the idea is to encourage quantity rather than quality at this stage. I want as many words (particularly adjectives!) written as possible on

the subject. Setting a short time limit works well with boys who like the competitive call. Then I ask them to count the amount of words, and we discover who wrote the most. The winner reads their list out. Now the second draft begins. I make – and we discuss – the following suggestions:

1. Take out any weak or unnecessary words.

2. Re-order the poem – does it work better in a different sequence?

3. Pair together any opposites (e.g. mellow teachers/angry teachers).

4. Look for alliteration (calm teachers/kind teachers).

5. Look for obvious rhymes (small dogs/tall dogs).

6. Think of a short introduction and an ending.

I explain that the poem need not rhyme, and that the repeated words give the poem its rhythm – and that you can still add to the poem at this late stage. Teachers themselves may have other comments or suggestions, depending on the recent literacy work undertaken in the classroom. When some of the second drafts are finished, pupils share them and we discuss them. The third draft consists of producing a final version, with proper spelling.

Ten Pin Bowling

Old Bowlers,
young bowlers,
smart bowlers,
raggedy bowlers,
anxious bowlers,
confident bowlers,
bowlers who bite their lips.

Bowlers in shorts,
bowlers in t-shirts,
bowlers in trainers,
bowlers who lose,
bowlers who win,
bowlers who like to score a strike.

Bowlers who are weak,
bowlers who are bolder,
I'd like to be a bowler
when I get older.

(by Timothy Hopper, Storrington First School, Storrington)

Picture This

Magazines, Sunday newspapers, catalogues, brochures and postcards are all useful sources of pictures. Children can be encouraged to collect images that interest and bring them in to class. Classes can attend art galleries or museums, and do initial brainstorm workshop activities on location, which can later be developed in the classroom.

Teachers can choose a picture (a painting, illustration or photograph) for a workshop, ideally poster-size, or could scan images onto an interactive whiteboard. Responses – scribed by the teacher – to some of the questions below can be developed into poems. The forms of poetry will depend on the material generated. Ideas connected with a sense of place or emotion may work well as free verse or as syllabic poetry such as haiku or tanka. If the image is of a person (or even a tree, river, cloud, mountain) the resulting poem could be a short free verse monologue poem in the voice of the person or the object.

- How would you describe this picture?
- How would you describe the mood or atmosphere?
- How does it make you feel?
- What happened before or after this picture?
- Who are the people in this picture? What are they doing? How do they feel at this moment? How do they feel about each other? What would they be saying if they were speaking? What thoughts are going through their minds? What will they do next? What question(s) would you like to ask these people?
- Where is this place? How does it feel to be there? Describe this place in terms of all the senses – such as sight, smell, sound and feel. What are the weather conditions? Is it hot, warm or cold? Is there a breeze blowing?
- When is this? What year? What time of year? What time of day?
- What is taking place – and, most importantly, why?

Another approach is to mix media, and teachers can play music while the class is discussing the picture and this will further help to bring out moods, atmospheres and ideas for writing.

Shapes of Things

See the poem 'Owls' on p. 31, 'Electric Guitars' on p. 102 and 'Fizz' on p. 79. Write a poem about something that has a simple shape – say a fish, a bird, a tree, a train or a car.
Or do a group shape poem display – such as weather display – in which you all do a shape poem: raindrops, rainbows, clouds, umbrellas, snowmen, the sun or puddles. Or, you could do different types of transport, or various animals – e.g. farm animals, animals in a wood or rainforest or fish in the ocean.

It doesn't matter whether what you end up with is a poem or a shape or anything, just so long as you have fun and aim at being inventive with shapes and words and language. Some of these shapes were created in recent workshops: stars, weather charts, champagne bottles, ghosts, faces, a Caribbean island, a piano keyboard and even Big Ben! Also see 'Musical Instruments' workshop on p. 65.

Show and Tell

Teacher-led activity: each child brings in something old from home that belongs/has belonged to a parent/grandparent/relation. Each child talks about the significance/background to the artefact. Children then either (a) write a free verse poem that tells the story behind the object or (b) write a poem in the voice of the object. With the latter, the poem could even be in the form of a a riddle: 'What am I? I'm . . .'

Speaking and Listening Workshop

Really, all creative writing activities in the primary classroom begin with talk in some way or other, but the following activities exploit talk and improvisation as a way of sourcing material for poetry.

'Overheard on a Saltmarsh' Workshop

Read through the poem on p. 116 a few times. In pairs, children adopt the characters of the nymph and the goblin and act out a range of possible scenarios:

- The goblin has stolen the beads.
- The goblin has something that the nymph would like.
- The nymph tricks the goblin into believing something.

Or children could invent their own scenarios. Children can be encouraged in their improvisations to emulate the poetic style of language used by the goblin – in phrases such as:

> They are better than stars or water,
> Better than voices of winds that sing.

When they have finished their improvisations, the children can write out one of their duologues as a piece in the same format as the original poem. Alternatively, children could choose two other fantasy characters to adopt.

Conversation poems

You could pick people you know, and write conversations between yourself and: your teacher, a friend, your brother and sister or member of your family. Or, you could pick something more unusual, such as conversations between the sun and the moon, two clouds, two animals or birds or fish, or a river and the sea.

You do not need to use speech marks, and can put each person speaking on alternate lines:

> You look dog tired.
>   Do I?
> You should take a cat nap.
>   Oh.

> (from 'Animal Instincts' by James Carter)

These poems can be improvised in pairs, and the results can be written down.

Further Improvisations in Pairs

In their twos, children decide which role they will take. Suggestions: teacher–pupil, parent–child, brother–sister or one of your own. Once you have decided upon your roles, one of you will begin with one of these lines:

> 'Why didn't you tell me about . . .'

> 'Why did you lie to me?'

> 'When did it happen?'

> 'How long have you known about . . .'

Or, have one child complaining or boasting or telling the other a secret. After the dialogue, each has to write a free verse poem in the voice of the character, discussing the conversation. You could even improvise some conversations onto cassette and write out transcripts and adapt these into poems.

Titles

Poets often recommend that you shouldn't decide upon a title until you are finishing off a poem. However, it can be fun writing to a set title. Here are some titles from existing poems you might wish to borrow for a poem of your own. You could also use the title as your opening line. When you have finished the poem, you could even change the title/opening line so that the poem is all your own work.

- 'The Nobody on the Hill' (Matthew Sweeney)
- 'Night School' (Philip Gross)
- 'The King of Cats Send a Postcard to his Wife' (Nancy Willard)
- 'Magic Story for Falling Asleep' (Nancy Willard)
- 'The Monster that Ate the Universe' (Roger Stevens)
- 'The Bully' (Adrian Mitchell)
- 'At the Bottom of the Garden' (Grace Nichols)
- 'Everything Changes' (Cicely Herbert)
- 'The River's Story' (Brian Patten)
- 'No!' (Thomas Hood)

Two Voices

Read through the poem 'Fireflies' by Paul Fleischman on p. 112 a few times. Look at the unusual structure of this poem. Write a piece like this poem for two voices – either on your own or as a pair. Other creatures you could choose: owls, eagles, dolphins, ladybirds, tigers, wolves, or an animal of your own choice. Or, it does not have to be an animal at all – perhaps ghosts or angels?. You could write a piece that includes actions/movements for a performance.

When I Grow Up

Based on 'You Can't Be That' by Prian Patten (p. 114). Each child writes one verse of a class 'conga poem' (free verse) in which they write about one particular occupation they would consider when they are older, but from both a positive and negative viewpoint. One child might choose to be an astronaut:

> I'd like to be . . . an astronaut
> it would be great:
> all that travelling
> all that excitement
> all that floating about in space
> and I'd really get to see the world
> and maybe visit other planets
> and I would be famous for ever and ever

But hang on . . .
I'd have to work very long hours
I'd spend months away from home
and it's quite dangerous, isn't it?
and what happens if something went wrong?

The whole class could perform their version of the poem in an assembly.

Photocopiable Pages

Reflections on Poetry

JOHN BETJEMAN: 'Poetry is the shortest way of saying things. It also looks nicer on the page than prose. It gives room to think and dream.'

VALERIE BLOOM: 'I see poetry as useful for making sense of the environment around you as well as the feelings inside you. Poets need to have heightened perception – they need to see, feel and experience things more vividly. They then bring their own experiences and imaginations together in such a way that the resulting poem can communicate to its reader. A good poem has a universality yet will speak individually to anyone who reads it. Poetry can sometimes be used as therapy. It can unearth a lot of buried emotions, and, as a result, can have a cleansing effect. It's not just the senses which are more sharply focused in poetry. Emotions are more keenly felt as well.'

JAMES CARTER: 'Poetry is language at its most playful and musical.'

PIE CORBETT: 'Poetry is a way of capturing and recreating our lives – a way of explaining the world to ourselves and ourselves to the world.'

JOHN FOSTER: 'Where do I get my ideas from? My answer to this question is that you get ideas for poems in three ways – from your own experience, from observation and from imagination. And every single word, even down to the last pronoun, counts. It matters in a poem whether you use, for example, "a" or "the". I spend a lot of time just improving single words to find the best one for the job. A message I spread to children is that you can actually spend up to half an hour working on just one single word.

'I'm often asked what poetry is and the only definition that I can come up with that actually works is that poetry is words patterned on a page. Also, poetry can be about any subject matter – for example, Michael Rosen has written a poem about a tube of toothpaste! Poetry can explore anything that writing can explore. What distinguishes it from prose is that it doesn't have to have a narrative element and it's patterned differently.'

TONY MITTON: 'If I had to sum it up in one sentence, I'd say that poetry is language dancing. For me, poetry comprises at least three main areas. First, there's the idea, the job that the poem is doing – what the content is saying. Next, there's the images, the pictures that the poem conjures. Finally, there's the music of the poem – the way the poem uses the sounds and rhythms of language.'

BRIAN MOSES: 'As Coleridge said, prose is words in the best order, poetry is the best words in the best order. I suppose because I'm attracted so much to music and the rhythms of music, I'm attracted to the rhythms of poetry and language. I love words and how poetry allows you to string words together in a variety of ways. For me, a poem is a snapshot giving you a brief glimpse, but a glimpse that is often so powerful that it can stay with you for ever. It enables you to look at the world in a different way.

'What I enjoy about poetry is that you can create a poem quickly and it's there and you feel good that you've done something that day – but a poem can take anything from five minutes to a year to write. A poem will initially take an hour or two – but I'm always tinkering away at it afterwards. Then I'll perform it and modify it. And then maybe perform it to a different audience and modify it again. Performances can help me to see if there are any flat points. Sometimes I'll start to write a poem, put it away for a couple of months, and then go back to it, and do a bit more to it – and it might take a year to get written. I don't think I ever quite know when a poem is finished. The only time I'll finally leave it alone is when it's published in a book.'

MICHAEL ROSEN: 'Poetry is like a devouring monster. It devours scraps of language from whenever and wherever it can: clichés, sports commentaries, letters, political speeches, science reports, newscasts, proverbs, shopping lists, other poems – any rhetorical device or linguistic structure can be and is used by poets' (from *Touches of Beauty* – Rosela Publications).

BENJAMIN ZEPHANIAH: 'What's poetry good for? It's good for capturing big emotions in a small, concise way, or, for taking little teeny things and stretching them out. It's good because Ted Hughes can do it, Bob Geldof can do it, Benjamin Zephaniah can do it – but Mr Brown at the allotment can also do it. It's the most democratic art form you can get. All you need is a pen and a piece of paper, and when it comes to oral poetry, you don't even need a pen and paper.'

Tips from Top Poets

VALERIE BLOOM: 'You need to "show" and not "tell". By this I mean that you need to actually "show" your reader things, not simply "tell" them about them. You need to let your reader experience things in your poem – that is, seeing or hearing or feeling something. These are what I refer to as "sense words". Take the sentence – "He was a very fat man." This is "telling". It is not very imaginative and does not conjure up much of an image. If we want to really "show" what the man is like we could say, "His stomach bulged over the waist of his trousers" – and then we understand he's fat. Likewise, "He was very upset" might be better expressed as "Tears streamed down his face." This way you are providing your reader with a clear visual image.'

JAN DEAN: 'It's very important to me to hear a poem out loud as I'm writing it. When I go into schools I tell children to trust their ears and to test their poems by reading them out loud. Something might look right on the page, but if you say it, it might not sound right.'

JOHN FOSTER: 'When is a poem finished? A poem is finished when every word counts and when every word sounds right. Even if I'm writing a non-rhyming poem, I'll read it aloud or at least say it through in my head to see if it is sounding right and every word is doing the job it should be doing.

'Children enjoy writing their own rhymes. But rhyming is difficult. In my workshops I'll tell children that if they want to rhyme, then fine, but they'll find it much harder than free verse.'

COLIN MACFARLANE: 'If you've written a first verse, say it over and over in your head so that the rhythm is fixed and you know the feel of it well – then carry on – with that first verse in the back of your mind.

'Be highly descriptive but beware of using too many adjectives or adverbs. Instead, find exactly the right adjective that you need. Also, if you are using adverbs too often it may mean that your verbs are weak and not expressive enough.'

ROGER MCGOUGH: 'One mistake people often seem to make with poetry is to try and describe something. I like poetry that comes at a subject from a different angle. It's a way of looking at something, and you can't force that, you have to let it happen.'

TONY MITTON: 'When you're writing poetry you have to be prepared to write rubbish as you go along, rubbish that you can get rid of later. You just have to keep going until you write something that you like. It's a bit like trudging through a desert until you find your oasis, finding a place where you want to be.

'If you want to write well you need to become an expert with words and language. You need to be as skilful with words as a painter is with paints or a composer is with sounds. You've got to care about every word, every pause, every last detail of what you put.

'My advice on titles? If it's a serious poem and you want to title it, try to look clearly at the poem and see what title suggests itself. If nothing comes, just be logical and say "What is this poem about?" Say it was about Stonehenge, then why not call it "Stonehenge"? Also, you might want to think about your reader and the fact that you are giving your title as a doorway into that poem for the reader, and that it helps to inform them what the poem is all about. If you were writing a metaphorical or playful poem about some rocks, you might not actually say in the piece what it is about, so you might need a title like "The Rocks" or "Seashore" to tell the reader what it really is about.

'Look at lots of poetry and try to find how many things a poem can be. Poems come in many shapes and sizes, many types and forms. If you find a poet or a kind of poetry you really like, get to know that poetry well. You may like to try writing like that yourself. It's all right, especially early on, to copy other writers occasionally. And the more you write, the more you'll develop a voice of your own.'

BRIAN MOSES: 'The first few lines are what hooks the reader, so the opening has got to make an impact and to encourage the reader to want to read on. It's like the first page of a novel – you want to read on because you've been intrigued somehow by what you've read. And a good ending can be one of many things. It can be a good idea that you saved till last to round off the poem, or something that sums up the poem in some way or a joke or even something unexpected.'

MATTHEW SWEENEY: 'Be like spies – keep your eyes and ears open for anything you see and hear that's interesting or different.'

The Journey of a Poem: Two Poets Talk Poetry

VALERIE BLOOM: 'First comes the idea. This can come in many forms, and may just be a word, a phrase or even a smell that sparks a memory which will then become the germ of an idea. I have to make notes on the idea straight away or else it will go. I have dozens of notepads scattered all over the house, as well as in every handbag. Some ideas come to me as I'm going off to sleep – so there's a pad on the bedside table!

'I'll write the idea down just as it comes. Sometimes the idea will be a whole verse or even a whole poem. I can compose a whole poem in my head – perhaps three or four stanzas – but I'll need to write it down quickly. How long ideas stay in a notebook will vary. At times I find that I can jump into writing the poem too early and really the idea needs to wait a little longer to incubate. Premature birth has been the cause of death of quite a few poems. Sometimes one idea will need to join up with another idea for the poem to take off, and the second idea could be a little way behind the first.

'I'm always leafing through my books of ideas for poems. If I have a spare minute to write I'll go through the books. If an idea leaps out at me and says 'Use me!' I'll start developing it. With prose pieces I work straight onto the computer, but with poems I work in the notebook first as I like to see the different drafts and stages that the pieces are going through. On the computer I've found that I might delete something that I later want to use, so I always begin poems in my notebooks now.

'At a much later stage I'll transfer to the computer, where I might make some further tweaks and changes or even move stanzas around. The title is usually the last thing to come – though I have a working title from the start. And the number of drafts will vary. Some poems – such as my very short ones – arrive almost complete so will need very few tweaks or polishing.

'I show new poems to my family for their responses. I'm always keen to hear what they have to say. My husband is an English teacher and he's actually had to teach my poetry at GCSE! My daughter is a very harsh critic. She gives my poems grades, and she'll make comments like 'A good effort!' So, having taken on board my family's responses I might make further changes and then I'll take the new poems into schools and perform them. During performance I will discover what works well and what doesn't and I will make more adjustments accordingly. Overall, it can take a very long time from that first idea to having a poem published.'

(See Valerie Bloom's poem 'The Visitor' on p. 50)

TONY MITTON: 'My shorter poems will come out in one sitting. With those poems I might hardly change anything – I'll just do a tweak or a twiddle to tighten the poem up a bit. But all my poems begin life in my notebooks. I write in cheap hardback lined paper notebooks. I carry them with me most of the time. In my notebooks I will often write and re-write. I scribble a lot in them. They're my own private place in which to be as playful as I want to be.

'I do a first draft or two of a poem in my notebook. Then I'll type it up onto the computer and print it out and work on it manually again. Then, I'll go back and rework the poem on the screen. I like that late stage of working with the poem on the computer as by then I'm feeling that the poem is pretty much finished. At that late stage I might make some crucial changes – such as moving verses about or adding new lines. I tend to spot any weaknesses in a poem at that stage.

'Some things I'll write direct onto the word processor – such as letters, stories for educational books – but hardly ever with poetry. It doesn't feel right with poetry. I love the pen in the hand on the paper. With longer, narrative poems – such as 'Anansi Meets Big Snake' – I plan. I make sure I've got the story sketched out for myself first, often in note form. I might write something like 'Girl loses ball. Ball drops in pond. Frog arrives.' – basically a plot summary.'

(See Tony Mitton's poem 'Anansi Meets Big Snake' on p. 38)

Forms of Poetry

ACROSTICS – poems in which, most frequently, the letters at the start of each line spell out a word:

Shows up every Christmas without fail
Always knows what you've asked for
Never forgets where you live
Takes nothing in return:
Ace guy

ALPHABET POEMS – a poem in which the 26 lines begin with each letter of the alphabet in turn, e.g.:

All
Birds
Can
Dance . . .

Some alphabet poems rhyme:

Alligator, beetle, porcupine, whale,
Bobolink, panther, dragonfly, snail . . .

BALLAD – a rhyming, performance poem that tells a story.

CALLIGRAM – a poem in which the look of the words represents the meaning. Examples:

TALL
curly
PROUD

FREE VERSE – poetry that does not rhyme or follow a set rhythm. Modern free verse is often written in everyday language.

KENNING – a form of list poem (usually non-rhyming) that provides a list of images and qualities of its subject. Animals are a popular theme with kennings; here is a short rhyming example of an elephant kenning:

A slow-walker
A time-taker
A deep-thinker
A big-shaker

LIMERICK – a humorous one-verse rhyming nonsense poem with an AABBA rhyme scheme.

LIST POEM – a poem that repeats a word or phrase at the beginning of each line or stanza, for example:

Write your name on a board with a chalk
Write your name in the air as you talk

NARRATIVE POEM: a poem that tells a story.

NONSENSE: Fun, usually rhyming poems that make little or no sense at all!

RAP – a rhyming poem with a strong rhythm, written in rhyming couplets, using modern language.

RIDDLE: a poem that gives the reader clues to guess what the subject may be.

I am in Ian – you'll find me in James
you'll find us in Susan – and just me in names
And I am in Tim – but also in him
we're all in Wendy – who are we?

SHAPE POEM: a poem in which the words form a specific shape. Also known as 'concrete poetry'. Example:

how
much
fizz
will
fit
into a
bottle?
well, at a
guess, I'd
say quite
a lottle

SONNET – a 14-line poem that often rhymes. Many sonnets are love poems.

SYLLABIC POETRY: HAIKU/TANKA/CINQUAINS – haiku is a form of poetry that originated in Japan and has 17 syllables in total. These syllables are divided into three lines as follows:

1st line: five syllables
2nd line: seven syllables
3rd line: five syllables

A haiku will give a short image or description. Example:

One little raindrop
a fragile silver planet
sitting on a leaf

Another syllabic poem is the cinquain – and has five lines of 22 syllables:

1st line: two syllables
2nd line: four syllables
3rd line: six syllables
4th line: eight syllables
5th line: two syllables

Example:

Heaven
must be like this:
warm sunshine all day long
nothing to do – nowhere to go
perfect!

Poetry Glossary

ALLITERATION AND ASSONANCE – Alliteration = where words begin with the same letters or sounds – 'table top', 'car keys', 'Anna's apple', 'green grass grew'. Assonance = where words near to each other in a line have the same sounds – 'green bean', 'new view'.

ANTHOLOGY – a book of poems by various poets often on the same theme, for example Christmas or shape poems. A COLLECTION is a book of poems by a single poet.

CLICHÉ – an overused and unoriginal phrase or description – 'as black as night'; 'as cold as ice'.

CONSONANCE – when endings of words close together have similar consonant sounds: 'The tick of the clock' or 'That night/we went out . . .'

COUPLET – two rhyming lines together.

DRAFTING AND EDITING – Drafting = doing different versions to improve and develop a piece of writing. Editing = checking a piece for spelling, grammar and punctuation.

FORM – the type of poem, such as rap or free verse or haiku.

IMAGERY – the pictures that a poem creates.

METAPHOR AND SIMILE – Simile = when you say one thing is *like* something else – 'as cunning as a fox', 'she felt trapped like a bird in a cage'. Metaphor = when you say one thing actually *is* something else – 'it's raining nails', 'the city is a jungle tonight'. Both are also known as 'figurative language'.

METER – a set, regular rhythm to a poem.

MONOLOGUE – a poem written in the voice of one person. A monologue can take the form of a rhyming poem, a rap or even a free verse poem.

NARRATIVE – the story that a poem tells.

ONOMATOPOEIA – words that mimic the sound they describe, such as hiss or pop.

PERSONIFICATION – a metaphor that compares something to a human being – 'the wind laughed', 'the moon shared its secrets with the sea'.

POINT OF VIEW – some poems can be told in the voice of a person or show the world as it is seen through one person's eyes; this is the 'point of view' of the poem.

RHYME – when the sounds at the end of a line agree with each other:

> Have you ever seen a sheet on a river *bed*?
> Or a single hair from a hammer's *head*?

A 'half-rhyme' is when words have similar but not identical sounds: fish/bit or house/round or clock/tick or hand/wand.

RHYTHM – the way that a poem is spoken: the way that the words work together to create a pattern of sounds.

STRUCTURE – how the poem is laid out, with a beginning, middle and an end.

SYLLABLE – a unit of sound in a word. Po/em has two syllables. Po/et/ry has three syllables. How many are there in your name/the place where you live?

THEME – the main subject(s) of a poem.

VERSE – a group of lines in a poem. Also known as a 'stanza'.

The First Draft

In a first draft –

DON'T WORRY ABOUT:

    spelling
    handwriting
    or even being too neat

GET ALL YOUR IDEAS DOWN ONTO PAPER:

    words
    phrases
    lines and verses
    title(s)
    rhymes
    images
    narrative
    conversations
    emotions/feelings

in fact, anything that comes to you – even if you are not sure that all the ideas will fit into that poem.

TRY NOT TO FORCE THE POEM. Take your time. It may take a few sittings to get the poem right.

DON'T WORRY about making each word, phrase and line perfect. You can change all that later.

KEEP THE FIRST DRAFT until you have finished the poem – you still might want to use some early ideas or refer back to this draft. Even if you put it onto computer, keep the manual copy.

DON'T EXPECT TOO MUCH of a first draft. It won't be perfect. Try to enjoy the writing.

DO FEEL FREE TO CROSS THINGS OUT – write over the top, put arrows in and so on. Just try not to rub anything out. You might want those ideas later!

DO SPEND TIME DAYDREAMING – good ideas can come this way. Take a break every now and then.

Crafting and Drafting Poems

When you are writing a poem there are many things to think about.
The questions below may help you to develop your poem.

LANGUAGE:

Do you repeat some words too often?

Are you using the right words and the best words you can?

Could you take some words out? (remember: less is more)

Is any of the phrasing awkward?

Are there too many over-used adjectives (nice, beautiful, lovely, etc.)?

Are you using clichés (unoriginal words or phrases) that could be changed?

Are you giving enough or too much detail?

Are you using metaphors or similes? Are there too many?

Do your rhymes work well? Are you using any words just for the sake of a rhyme?

IMAGE:

Are you painting a full picture for your reader?

Are your descriptions too vague or unclear?

Are you 'showing' or 'telling'?

STRUCTURE:

Do you have a good beginning, middle and end?

Does the opening grab your attention and make you want to go on?

Have you got the best possible opening line or stanza?

RHYTHM:

Do the words, phrases and lines flow?

How well does it read out loud?

Is the rhythm working well overall?

Do you keep to the same rhythm throughout?

GENERAL:

Are your lines the right length?

If it is a free verse poem – could the lines be shorter?

Should the poem be in a different form?

Is the poem too complicated?

Is the title right? Is the title too obvious? Is the title doing its job – try a couple of other titles, then pick the best one.

Is the poem original in any way?

Is there anything in the poem that you don't need?

Does the poem do what you want it to do?

Will the poem make sense to a reader?

How will a reader respond to this?

What are the strengths and weaknesses of the poem?

THE NEXT STEP:

Read the poem out loud – or ask a friend to read it to you. Listen to every word and every phrase.

How could it be improved?

What needs to be done next?

If you have gone through the checklist and you are not sure what needs to be done next, leave your poem for a while and come back to it later. This quote might help you to decide if you have finished working on a poem:

'A poem is finished when every word counts and when every word sounds right. Even if I'm writing a non-rhyming poem, I'll read it aloud or at least say it through in my head to see if it is sounding right and every word is doing the job it should be doing.' (John Foster)

Stage

Developing *speaking and listening* skills through performance poetry

(including CD)

Why Perform Poetry?

Poetry is arguably the best medium for performance in the classroom as most poems are short, and do not take the time and studying that a drama text can. Added to this, much of the poetry written for children nowadays works best of all when performed.

Children need to hear and read and discuss poetry as part of their weekly literacy activities – as poetry will inform, nurture and develop their speaking and listening skills as well as their understanding, awareness and appreciation of language in general.

To perform a poem is much more than simply reading the words. It is the job of a performance to communicate the piece to an audience. A performance involves using the appropriate pace and voice, bringing out the mood, tone and atmosphere of the poem, and above all, bringing the poem to life.

Often, when people perform poems they have learnt the piece by heart and this makes all the difference. Poems that have been learnt and then performed have a greater vitality. And perhaps the hardest part of a performance is letting go – and not allowing yourself to feel self-conscious or awkward, and though this may seem a more adult condition, many children experience this too. Finding the confidence to let go, and letting the tone and subject matter of the poem dictate will come with practice and experience, encouragement and support.

It has been proved that performing poetry can help to develop children's oracy skills, as Penny Hollander, AST teacher and Year 5/6 teacher at Ewelme (C of E) Primary School explains:

> During the past four years we have developed the concept of performance poetry as a means of developing children's self-esteem and confidence in public speaking as well as encouraging the use of speaking and listening skills. We have seen this area as an extremely important component of school life that is inclusive, regardless of age and ability. It has also introduced the children to a wide range of poems, old and new.
>
> The first poem we performed was Clement Clark Moore's 'A Visit from St Nicholas' as part of a Christmas production. All pupils from ages 5 to 11 participated in this, with some of the youngest children learning it before the older ones! Some able pupils helped those who found it more difficult. It was wonderful to see that for the first time in her life a Year 6 pupil with quite severe special educational needs was able to stand and recite the whole poem with everyone else, and, what is more, she knew she could do it.
>
> Since then our range of perfromance poetry has extended from classic poems such as 'Hiawatha' and 'The Pied Piper of Hamelin' to humorous ones like 'The Owl and the Pussycat' and 'King John's Christmas'. We even performed 'All of Us Knocking at the Stable Door' during a Christmas service in church. Latterly, we have moved into rap, and Tony Mitton's 'Little Red Rap' was part of a QCA video *Working with gifted and talented pupils: Key Stages 1 & 2 English and Mathematics*.

Penny Hollander's Year 5/6 class are featured on the accompanying CD, tracks 5 to 9.

This part of *Page to Stage* aims to encourage children to be critical readers of poems and to read text closely. But it also seeks to give teachers – and ultimately children – a range of stimulating activities in which they can perform poetry as individuals, as groups or as a whole class – either in the classroom, or in assemblies or in school concerts. When working in this way as an ensemble of performers, children become a 'poetry choir' – each performing a variety of roles – perhaps taking a lead role, or as part of a chorus, or even contributing some live music to the performance.

Some children are more confident with oral activities and may relish the opportunity to read poems and to bring them to life rather than sit down and write their own pieces. Now that drama is rarely more than the Christmas play or panto, poetry can give teachers the chance to engage in a wealth of speaking and listening activities, to consider text in performance and to bring out performance skills that would otherwise lie dormant or never be used at all. And actually, with some of the pieces in this book the boundaries between verse and dramatic text are blurred – Harold Munro's 'Overheard on a Saltmarsh' and Paul Fleischman's 'Fireflies' are poems that can be performed as short dramatic pieces.

On a personal note, perhaps the best compliment I have had as a performance poet was from a Year 6 boy in a school near Coventry. He said, 'When you perform it's like we're inside the poem with you.' Wow! – what a lovely thing to be told. And what an astute and indeed poetic way of describing the experience of listening to poetry being performed. In fact, the rest of this part of the book is dedicated to that very thing – encouraging and developing children as performers, as speakers and listeners – so that they too can invite their audiences to be 'inside' poems with them.

DfES Recommendations for Speaking and Listening

The range of oracy-related activities in *Page to Stage* (from individual poetry performances to group performances to whole class performances) will help classes to reach DfES expectations with regard to speaking and listening – as detailed in the DfES document *Speaking, Listening, Learning: Working with Children in Key Stages 1 and 2*:

[At] Key Stages 1 and 2 children are expected to make progress in:

- sustaining speaking and listening
- contributing in a range of ways
- adapting to different circumstances and contexts with independence and confidence
- talking explicitly about speaking and listening.

A number of speaking and listening objectives as advocated in the DfES document are implicit within many of the poetry performance workshops that are presented in this part of the book, including:

Characteristics of children's talk –
Children:

- take turns and speak one at a time
- speak clearly and audibly
- respond appropriately to other speakers
- sustain contributions
- use tentative/exploratory language when thinking something through
- formulate and express opinions
- ask questions
- [use] good vocabulary
- use facial expressions and gestures to emphasise points
- use a range of ways to express themselves
- make eye contact with listeners
- use talk to clarify their ideas
- putting thoughts into words and sharing in groups
- respond to others' contributions by adding or elaborating on them or putting across another view

- speak in range of contexts, including – to different audiences, such as the class, the teacher, other adults; for different purposes, such as recounting events and telling stories . . .

When listening, children are:
- hearing models of language in use
- learning about how speakers use gesture, volume, tone.

And yet another reference in the document, this time to drama, equally relevant to performance poetry is:

Children need to learn to respond to their own and others' performances, commenting constructively . . .

Role(s) of the Teacher

With poetry performance workshops, the teacher has a variety of roles to play:

- A *model* of language – performing a variety of poems to children, and in a range of voices/tones, so that children can in turn emulate these.
- A *coach* – to support children with their own performances to feed back and respond, and to encourage children to evaluate their own performances and to contribute ideas to feed back to their peers.
- A *chair* – to oversee performances, to help children choose suitable poems.
- A *critical reader* of poems – one that helps children to read and enjoy but also analyse and appreciate poems in terms of:
  form (the type of poem/point of view/use of language – the 'music' of the poem – such as rhythms and rhymes, alliteration and assonance/use of metaphors and similes) as well as –
  content (themes/messages/images/idea of the poem/tone and atmosphere).
- A *director* – to guide, motivate and direct individuals as well as groups and class ensembles.

In one respect, performing poetry should be a less daunting task for teachers than creative writing as there is already something – a text – to begin with. A poem already comes with clues about performance – in the choice of the poet's words, the subject matter, the phrasing, the rhythm, the tone, the style and so on.

Running a Poetry Performance Workshop

In the same way that a poem is never fully written in one sitting or workshop, a performance of a poem will develop and evolve over a number of workshops. However, a performance workshop is very different in nature, purpose and structure to a writing workshop. Whereas a writing workshop begins with blank sheets of paper and a search for ideas, a text – or the search for a text – precedes a performance workshop.

It is worth mentioning at this point that not all poems are meant to be performed. Some are written to live on the page and to be read silently and heard only in the mind's ear – these are often referred to as 'page poems'.

A poem may be chosen by the child or the teacher. Poems for a class poetry performance may stem from a variety of sources:

- poems written by the children – on one topic or a range of topics
- published poems on a specific topic – the school, a season, friends/family, something that relates to a class topic – sourced from either poetry collections (single author) or poetry anthologies (many poets)
- poems by a poet that has visited the school
- poems for one voice/two voices/a number of voices
- poems in a specific form/style – e.g. raps, free verse poems, funny poems, autobiographical poems, etc.
- poems for a special occasion – retirement of teacher/headteacher, a centenary of the school, etc.

Stages of a Workshop

(See Section 2 – 'Preparing Poems for Performance' on specific issues to consider in workshops.)

1. *Teacher* reads through the poem a few times to model a reading – the text is displayed on the board and/or with photocopies of the poem given to the class. If teachers are using poetry recordings instead, they will play the cassette/CD at this point.
2. *Class/groups of children* read along – ideally a number of times.
3. *Teacher* points out various aspects of the poem – the form, rhythm, rhymes, themes and so on (see 'Talking Poetry' below) – children annotate the poem on their photocopy sheets.
4. *Teacher/class* discuss ways that the poem can be spoken and orchestrated, and discuss issues such as dynamics/pace/tone and whether to use music or actions (for all of these issues see 'Preparing Poems for Performance' section) – again children make notes on their photocopy sheets.
5. *Children* – now in groups and with allocated roles/verses/lines – try out and experiment with the poem; teacher and other children feed back; children continue to make notes on their photocopy sheets, and develop the performance.

The last three stages will carry on over a number of workshops until the children have learnt the poems by heart and the poems are ready to be performed. Teachers can video or tape record rehearsals to give further feedback to the children.

Staging a Poetry Concert

Poetry concerts may be held in a variety of places within the school:

- in class, for a small audience
- in the hall for a KS1 or KS2 assembly or for the whole school or for parents and visitors
- alternatively, a KS2 class may visit a KS1 class or department to give a poetry performance (or vice versa).

There will need to be a 'dress rehearsal' so that children know the running order of poems, and how the performance as a whole will be introduced, sequenced and concluded, and where individuals will stand/perform.

Further issues to be considered:

- Individual children can introduce the performance as a whole – as well as specific poems.
- Actions to accompany poems may be incorporated into performances.

- If classes are going to ask the audience to join in, this needs to be established and scripted so that the performers know what to say to the audience at the appropriate time.
- Musical instruments may be used to accompany the poems – to give either a rhythm or atmosphere before or during the pieces.

Examples of different types of poetry concerts:

Year 2 Poetry Concert – theme: 'Animals'

- Two children introduce the assembly.
- Whole class performs 'The Owl and the Pussycat' by Edward Lear.
- Individual children perform their own animal poems, such as riddles or kennings.
- Whole class perform 'Leap Like a Leopard' by John Foster (from *Doctor Proctor and Other Rhymes*: OUP 1998) and with actions – teacher/class demonstrate actions for audience to join in.
- Two children thank the audience for listening.

Year 4 Poetry Concert – theme: 'Nonsense Poems'

- Two children introduce the assembly.
- Whole class performs 'Jabberwocky' by Lewis Carroll (as a rap with backing music).
- Two small groups of boys and girls perform 'World of Weird' by James Carter (with actions).
- A pair of boys and girls perform nonsense poems they have written – each poem has a chorus that the audience/rest of class join with.
- Whole class performs Spike Milligan's 'On the Ning Nang Nong' (*The Works* – Paul Cookson Pan Macmillan) – a large version of the poem is reproduced on an OHP.
- Two children thank the audience for listening.

Year 5 Poetry Concert – theme: 'School'

- One child introduces the assembly.
- Whole class perform 'Please Mrs Butler' by Allan Ahlberg (from *Please Mrs Butler* by Allan Ahlberg – Puffin 1983).
- A small group perform 'The Secret Lives of Teachers' by Brian Moses (from *The Secret Lives of Teachers* by Brian Moses – Pan Macmillan 1997).
- Small group perform own free verse poem about the class teacher.
- Whole class perform 'Year 5' rap written by the whole class; audience join in on chorus – poem accompanied by small percussion section.
- One child thanks the audience for listening.

Year 6 Poetry Concert – theme 'Forms of Poetry' (all own compositions)

- One child introduces the theme of the assembly.
- Individual children perform atmospheric haiku poems with background music.
- Small groups perform their own limericks.
- Individual children perform some quiet free verse poems – full of imagery/metaphor – some with music.
- Individual children show/read shape poems (large versions).
- Whole class perform their own poetry rap – a rap that lists all the forms of poetry.
- One child thanks the audience for listening.

Talking Poetry

Either before you begin writing or performing poems with your class, or maybe as a moment away from the creative process, you can take time to discuss various aspects of poetry:

- What is and isn't poetry?
- Is poetry like other forms of writing? As Michael Rosen has said, 'Poems are jokes, lessons, speeches, complaints, boasts, hopes, dreams, rumours, insults, gossip, memories, lists' to name but a few! What else is poetry similar to?
- How do you feel about poetry? Why?
- What do you like/dislike about poetry?
- Do you write poems at home? Why? Are they different to the ones you write at school?
- Do you prefer writing poems or prose? Why?
- What do you think is the difference between poetry and prose?
- When is an idea best served as a poem or as prose?
- What can a poem do that other forms of writing can't do?
- Why do you think more people choose to read prose and non-fiction than poetry?
- What is your favourite type/form of poetry?
- How many poets can you name?
- Do you know any poems off by heart?

Classes could read through the following sections of this book to stimulate discussion: 'What is Poetry?'/'Reflections on Poetry'/'The Journey of a Poem: Two Poets Talk Poetry'/'Tips From Top Poets'. See also the section 'Note It' later in this part of the book for discussion points/questions that can applied to poems – including those in this book/CD.

1

Anthology of Performance Poems (with performance notes)

'Shooting Stars' by James Carter (featured on the CD track 1)

'The Dark' by James Carter (featured on the CD track 2)

'World of Weird' by James Carter (featured on the CD track 3)

'Electric Guitars' by James Carter (featured on the CD track 4)

'Places in the World' by Red Grammer (performed by Ewelme C of E Primary School on the CD track 5)

'Fuss Fuss Fuss or the Goldilocks Rap' by James Carter (performed by Ewelme C of E Primary School on the CD track 6)

The Witches from Shakespeare's *Macbeth* (edited extracts from Acts I and IV – performed by Ewelme C of E Primary School on the CD track 9)

'Red Boots On' by Kit Wright

'Fireflies' by Paul Fleischman

'You Can't Be That' by Brian Patten

'Overheard on a Saltmarsh' by Harold Monro

'Jabberwocky' by Lewis Carroll

Other poems featured in *Page to Stage* that are suitable for performance:

'Anansi Meets Big Snake' by Tony Mitton (p. 38)

'Hedgehog Hiding at Harvest in Hills Above Monmouth' by Helen Dunmore (p. 49)

'Straining' by Michael Rosen (p. 19)

Limericks by Edward Lear (p. 40)

'The Visitor' by Valerie Bloom (p. 50)

'A Girl's Head' by Katherine Gallagher (p. 18)

'Talking Time' by James Carter (p. 55)

'Sorry Sorry Sorry' by James Carter (p. 42)

The Shooting Stars

That night
we went out in the dark
and saw the shooting stars
was one of the best nights ever

It was as if someone
was throwing paint
across the universe

The stars just kept coming
and we 'oohed' and 'aahed'
like on bonfire night

And it didn't matter
they weren't real stars –
just bits of dust on fire
burning up in the atmosphere

And we stayed out there for ages
standing on this tiny planet
staring up at the vast cosmos

And I shivered
with the thrill
of it all

James Carter

Performance Notes for 'The Shooting Stars' (CD track 1)

Read the poem through while listening to the recorded version on the CD. This version is performed by one voice. The recording has sound effects all the way through and atmospheric music at the start. Other possible ways of performing 'The Shooting Stars' include:

- A small group performs the piece – with individual voices taking a stanza each – or, stanzas are spoken in unison by pairs or the whole group.
- Actions could be introduced. For instance, throughout, the performer(s) could look upwards from time to time, as well as:

  'It was as if someone/was throwing paint/across the universe' – throw one arm upwards, as if throwing something through the air.
  'Just bits of dust on fire/burning up in the atmosphere' – with one finger trace the falling of a star across the sky.

- Children could compose a short piece of music – say with glockenspiels and soft percussion instruments (cabassas, rain sticks) to introduce and conclude the poem. The music could even be played very softly during the poem.

Being a quiet, reflective poem, it needs to be spoken softly – and could even be done in a whispery voice. Throughout, the poem needs to be slow, but some lines/stanzas could be paused or slowed down further.

NB: If 'Shooting Stars' is to be performed by more than one child, the final stanza would have to change to the first person plural:

And *we* shivered
with the thrill
of it all

The Dark

Why are we so afraid of the dark?
It doesn't bite and doesn't bark
Or chase old ladies round the park
Or steal your sweeties for a lark

And though it might not let you see
It lets you have some privacy
And gives you time to go to sleep
Provides a place to hide or weep

It cannot help but be around
When beastly things make beastly sounds
When back doors slam and windows creek
When cats have fights and voices shreek

The dark is cosy, still and calm
And never does you any harm
In the loft, below the sink
It's somewhere nice and quiet to think

Deep in cupboards, pockets too
It's always lurking out of view
Why won't it come out till it's night?
Perhaps the dark's afraid of light

James Carter

Performance Notes for 'The Dark' (CD track 2)

Read the poem through while listening to the recorded version on the CD. This version is performed by one voice. Other possible ways of performing 'The Dark' include:

- An ensemble – a pair/small group/whole class performs the poem. The poem could be chanted in unison, or small numbers of children/individuals could take on specific verses.
- Actions could be done at certain points, for example:

  'Or chase old ladies round the park' – run on the spot.
  'Or steal your sweeties for a lark' – grab something in the air and pop it in your mouth.
  'It lets you have some privacy' – hide your face behind your hands.

- 'The Dark' is a cheeky, playful poem and this tone needs to be brought out in performance. Do not be afraid to go a little bit over the top when saying some lines.
- Although there is a strong rhythm to the piece, do pause or slow down on certain lines/phrases for effect.
- A small group of children could compose a haunting, menacing piece of music to open/conclude the poem – suitable instruments would include violins, cellos and keyboards and drums/cymbals with beaters.

World of Weird

In the world of Weird
all the girls wear beards
and the boys keep bees in their beds
the girls dig holes and live like moles
and the boys grow trees on their heads

In the world of Weird
all the hamsters hum
and the hedgehogs whistle to their wives
the moles grow curls and live like girls
and the bees keep boys in their hives

In the world of Weird
all the oranges are blue
and the lemons are as sweet as can be
bananas are round, and grow in the ground
or down at the bottom of the sea

In the world of Weird
all the fish can fly
and the chips are fried in lakes
the dogs love cats: with sauce, of course –
served up on silver plates

Now how do you get
to the world of Weird? –
where is it? where is it? where?
hop on a bee – pop over the sea
then give us a call when you're there!

James Carter

Performance Notes for 'World of Weird' (CD track 3)

Read the poem through while listening to the recorded version on the CD. This version is performed by one voice and has sound effects on the voice at specific points. Other possible ways of performing 'World of Weird' include:

- An ensemble – group/whole class perform the poem as a rhythmic chant.

- Because there is reference to boys/girls in the first two stanzas, certain lines could be taken by girls and others by boys. One method:

All: 'In the World of Weird'
Boys: 'All the girls wear beards'
Girls: 'and the boys keep bees in their beds'
Boys: 'the girls dig holes and live like moles'
Girls: 'and the boys grow trees on their heads'

From there, lines could be swapped in this way for the rest of the poem.

- Actions can be undertaken at various points, for example:

'all the girls wear beards' – children stroke their chins
'and the boys grow trees on their heads' – children spread out their hands above their heads

- A small band of musicians could compose an introductory piece – making strange sounds on their instruments. Keyboards often have a range of unusual sound effects that would be ideal for this purpose.

NB: the recording has an extra piece of comic dialogue after the final verse. This does not have to be included in a performance.

Electric Guitars

I like electric guitars:
played mellow or moody
frantic or fast – on CDs
or tapes, at home or in
cars – live in the streets
at gigs or in bars.
I like
electric
guitars:
played
choppy
like
reggae
or angry
like
rock or
chirpy
like
jazz or
strummy
like
pop or
heavy
like
metal – it
bothers
me not.
I like electric guitars:
their strings and their straps
and their wild wammy bars – their
jangling and twanging and funky
wah-wahs – their fuzz boxes,
frets and multi-effects –
pick-ups, machine
heads, mahogany necks
– their plectrums, their wires,
and big amplifiers. I like electric
guitars: played loudly, politely – dully
or brightly – daily or nightly – badly
or nicely. I like electric guitars:
bass, lead and rhythm –
I basically dig 'em –
I like ele
c
t
r
i
c
g
u
i
t
a
r
s

James Carter

Performance Notes for 'Electric Guitars' (CD track 4)

Read the poem through while listening to the recorded version on the CD. This version is performed by one voice and has electric guitars played in a variety of styles throughout the recording.

To date, this poem has been performed in classes in a number of ways:

- As one person performing the poem while playing the guitar to certain lines (for example, 'played choppy like reggae' or 'angry like rock').
- By two people – one doing the words and the other playing the guitar parts.

If you are going to play the guitar during the poem, you need to decide which guitar riffs or chords you will play during the piece. You could listen to the CD recording and copy these or listen to some CDs for ideas – or even make up some of your own.

Another way would be for an ensemble or individual to chant the poem without guitars at all.

And a fun alternative would be to 'sing' the guitar parts and play air guitars!

Places in the World

These are places in the world . . .

Some you know and some you don't
some you'll visit and some you won't
some are near and some are far
some sound exotic like Zanzibar
'cause these are places in the world

Bombay, Cape May, Mandalay, Baffin Bay
Baghdad, Leningrad, Ashkabad, Trinidad
L.A., Norway, Paraguay, Monterey
Singapore, Ecuador, Bangalore, Baltimore
these are places in the world

Fiji, Sicily, Nagasaki, Tennessee
Cairo, Quito, Borneo, Idaho
Taiwan, Dijon, Saigon, Teheran
Guatemala, Oklahoma, Argentina, North Dakota
these are places in the world

Some are new, some are old
some are hot and some are cold
some are low and some are high
some are wet and some are dry
'cause these are places in the world

Glasgow, Oslo, Fresno, Tsingtao
Falkland, Auckland, Yucatan, Disneyland
Libya, Namibia, Romania, Pennsylvania
Bora Bora, Walla Walla, Costa Rica, Bratislava
these are places in the world

Krakow, Changchow, Moscow, Tokelau
Dominique, Pikes Peak, Mozambique, Bitter Creek
Warsaw, Moose Jaw, Saskatoon, Cameroon
Haifa, Mecca, Bethlehem, Jerusalem
these are places in the world

High on the mountain, down on the plain
deep in the jungle in the middle of the rain
children laugh and children play
everywhere, everyday
'cause these are places in the world

*Song lyric by Red Grammer, from Teaching Peace Teacher's Guide, Red Note
Records, 5049 Orangeport Road, Brewerton New York, 13029 USA*

Performance Notes for 'Places in the World' (CD track 5)

This is a song lyric, performed on the CD as a poem. Read through the lyric while listening to the recorded version on the CD. This version has been done with all the voices in unison. Other possible ways of performing 'Places in the World' include:

- Either individuals or small groups doing the introduction/main verses (those verses that list the place names) and the whole class does the choruses.
- In those verses that list the place names, each of the place names could be said by a different child in turn. For instance, with verse 2:

Child A says 'Bombay'
Child B says 'Cape May'
Child C says 'Mandalay'
Child D says 'Baffin Bay'

and so on throughout the verse. Other verses could be either done in unison, or broken down to individual phrases as demonstrated above.

- The pace could be varied. For the place name verses, these could be done slightly bolder and faster, and the other verses could be softer and slower.
- The final verse could become gradually louder or the last few lines could be repeated for effect.
- Some children in the class could act as a percussion band, laying down a slow, steady rhythm throughout the poem.

Fuss Fuss Fuss or The Goldilocks Rap

Hey everybody, listen, yo!
here's a tale you might just know
it's all about the 3 Bears 3
and the fussiest girl you ever did see
who went by the name of Little Miss G

Now G was out in the woods one day
when after a while she lost her way
and deeper and deeper into the wood
she followed the smell of something good

Soon she came to a dreamy cottage
and three hot bowls of creamy porridge -

Fuss Fuss Fuss!

one too lumpy, one too hot
but one just right – she scoffed the lot!

Fuss Fuss Fuss!

Next 3 chairs – and two weren't right
the other she broke – it served her right!

Fuss Fuss Fuss!

Next 3 beds, it was number 3
where G took a nap so peacefully

Fuss Fuss Fuss!

The bears came back before too long
crying 'What the ding dong's going on?!?'
and finding G in the tiny bed
it made those 3 Bears 3 see red

'Hey Goldie girl, you keep it real –
you can't just barge in here and steal
our food!' – you go and cook some more
you lazybod – you know the score

Never before in the dreamy cottage
had tastier bowls of creamy porridge
been cooked (by the bears or anyone)
so the bears said, 'G – it'd be such fun

to open a diner!' they did, it was cool
and G's food made those wood folk drool
and the fussiest girl you ever did see – went
Fuss Fuss Fuss!

well, no actually –

the fussiest girl you ever did see
cooked porridge ever after (quite happily)

James Carter

Performance Notes for 'Fuss Fuss Fuss' (CD track 6)

Read the poem through while listening to the recorded version on the CD. Note how the poem is orchestrated, and how some sections are done by individuals or a small group of voices, and elsewhere it is performed by the whole class. 'Fuss Fuss Fuss' is a rap poem – a playful, fun retelling of the 'Goldilocks' fairy tale and will need to be lively and spirited – but fairly slow and with a steady tempo.

Other possible ways of performing 'Fuss Fuss Fuss' include:

*   Performing the poem as a group or class in unison, as for 'Places in the World'.
*   The poem is spoken by one voice, with perhaps a group of voices for the 'Fuss Fuss Fuss!' chorus as well as the verse that begins 'Hey Goldie girl . . .'.
*   The poem is performed by a small group that takes a verse or two each, for example:

Child A: verse 1
Child B: verse 2
Child C: verse 3

and so on – with all the performers joining in for the 'Fuss Fuss Fuss' chants and possibly the 'Hey Goldie girl . . .' verse.
*   Consider actions. Examples:

'Hey everybody, listen, yo!' – beckon to audience with a hand
'three bears three' – hold up three fingers on right hand and then left hand.
'followed the smell of something good' – those not speaking at this point can inhale deeply as if smelling the porridge.
'one too lumpy, one too hot/but one just right – she scoffed the lot!' mimic the eating of porridge – with the first two bowls feign disgust, with the third, smile.

*   Some children in the class could act as a percussion band, laying down a slow, steady rhythm throughout the poem.

The Witches

from Shakespeare's *Macbeth* (edited extracts from Acts I and IV)

FIRST WITCH: When shall we three meet again,
                      In thunder, lightning, or in rain?

SECOND WITCH: When the hurlyburly's done;
                      When the battle's lost and won.

FIRST WITCH: Where the place?

SECOND WITCH: Upon the heath.

THIRD WITCH: There to meet with Macbeth.

ALL: Fair is foul, and foul is fair;
                      Hover through the fog and filthy air.

FIRST WITCH: Round about the cauldron go:
                      In the poisoned entrails throw
                      Toad that under cold stone
                      Days and nights has thirty-one.

ALL: Double, double, toil and trouble;
                      Fire burn and cauldron bubble.

SECOND WITCH: Fillet of a fenny snake:
                      In the cauldron boil and bake
                      Eye of newt, and toe of frog,
                      Wool of bat, and tongue of dog.

ALL: Double, double, toil and trouble;
                      Fire burn and cauldron bubble.

THIRD WITCH: Finger of birth-strangl'd babe,
                      Ditch-deliver'd by a drab, –
                      Make the gruel thick and slab.

ALL: Double, double, toil and trouble;
                      Fire burn and cauldron bubble.

SECOND WITCH: By the pricking of my thumbs,
                      Something wicked this way comes:
                      Open, locks, whoever knocks!

Performance Notes for 'The Witches' (CD track 9)

Read the text through while listening to the recorded version on the CD. This version is performed by three girls.

Out of context of the play, not all of this text will make full sense. In performances, children could begin at 'Round about the cauldron go' – and all the children will need to know is that these are three evil witches casting a magic spell. There are many simplified versions of Shakespeare's play available which will give the entire story in prose or as a reduced drama text.

Additional ways of performing this text include:

- Three boys (or combination of boys/girls) adopt the roles of the witches.
- Rather than three individuals, have three small groups, even mixed groups (boys/girls) of children.
- Perform the piece as a whole class.
- Children could write their own additional spells and verses and add these to the text (see related writing activity, p. 63).

Red Boots On

Way down Geneva
all along vine
deeper than the snow drift
love's eyes shine:

Mary Lou's walking
in the winter time.

She's got

*Red boots on, she's got
red boots on
kicking up the winter
till the winter's gone.*

So

Go by Ontario
look down Main
if you can't find Mary Lou
come back again

Sweet light burning
in winter's flame.

She's got

*Snow in her eyes, got
a tingle in her toes
and new red boots on
wherever she goes.*

So

All around Lake Street
up by St Paul
quicker than the white wind
love takes all:

Mary Lou's walking
in the big snow fall.

She's got

*Red boots on, she's got
red boots on
kicking up the winter
till the winter's gone.*

Kit Wright

Performance Notes for 'Red Boots On'

'Red Boots On' is a very popular performance poem in primary schools. There are a number of ways the poem can be performed, including:

- By one voice, or a pair of voices or by a small group or the whole class. With pairs, children could take a verse each and come together for the chorus sections. Likewise, small groups/whole classes could break the verses down into pairs/threes doing the verses and all come together for the choruses. Or, a whole class could chant the poem in unison.
- Lines in certain stanzas could be spoken by individual children. For example:

  Child 1: 'Go by Ontario'
  Child 2: 'Look down Main'
  Child 3: 'if you can't find Mary Lou'
  Child 4: 'come back again'

  This pattern could be repeated for the other verses.
- The final chorus could be done twice, with the second building to a crescendo.
- Actions could be introduced, for example:

  'Red boots on, she's got/red boots on' – point with both hands down to feet
  'kicking up the winter/till the winter's gone.' – kick out with feet as if walking through snow

This poem has a real uplifting, joyful feel to it and it needs to be performed with much enthusiasm and gusto! But the rhythm needs to be kept at a steady, medium tempo.

Fireflies

(a poem for two voices)

Light	Light is the ink we use
Night is our parchment	Night
	We're fireflies
fireflies flitting	flickering
	flashing
fireflies glimmering	fireflies gleaming
glowing	
Insect calligraphers practising penmanship	Insect calligraphers
	copying sentences
Six-legged scribblers of vanishing messages,	Six-legged scribblers
	fleeting graffiti
Fine artists in flight adding dabs of light	Fine artists in flight
	bright brush strokes
Signing the June nights as if they were paintings	Signing the June nights as if they were paintings
	We're fireflies
flickering fireflies fireflies.	flickering fireflies.

Paul Fleischman

Performance Notes for 'Fireflies'

There are a number ways the poem can be performed, including:

- By two individual children
- Two groups of children.

The poem calls for a very tight performance, and will need much rehearsing for either a pair or groups of children to say their words in sync.

Do copies of this poem. Draw a line between the two voices, so children can clearly tell which part they are adopting. Even use a colour highlight pen to further distinguish between the two parts.

When reading through, children can consider:

- Tone – this is a magical poem and the voices must reflect this.
- Dynamics – which words/phrases should be spoken softly or whispered.
- Pace – slow throughout, but pick up the pace slightly as the poem develops, then slow down again at the end of the poem. Practise to a steady beat (claps or tapping feet), but lose this in performance as it will jar with the magical atmosphere of the poem.
- Actions – such as with the line 'is the ink' – write in the air with a finger; and 'is our parchment' – spread out hands like a book. Children could work out actions and movements for the entire poem so that it becomes a short dramatic piece/dance.

You Can't Be That

I told them:
when I grow up
I'm not going to be a scientist
or someone who reads the news on TV.
No, a million birds will fly through me.
I'M GOING TO BE A TREE!

They said,
You can't be that. No, you can't be that.

I told them:
when I grow up
I'm not going to be an airline pilot,
a dancer, a lawyer or an MC.
No, huge whales will swim in me.
I'M GOING TO BE AN OCEAN!

They said,
You can't be that. No, you can't be that.

I told them:
I'm not going to be a DJ,
a computer programmer, a musician or beautician.
No, streams will flow through me, I'll be the home of eagles;
I'll be full of nooks, crannies, valleys and fountains.
I'M GOING TO BE A RANGE OF MOUNTAINS!

They said,
You can't be that. No, you can't be that.

I asked them:
just what do you think I am?
Just a child, they said.
and children always become
at least one of the things
we want them to be.

They do not understand me.
I'll be a stable if I want, smelling of fresh hay,
I'll be a lost glade in which unicorns still play.
They do not realise I can fulfil any ambition.
They do not realise among them
walks a magician.

Brian Patten

Performance Notes for 'You Can't Be That'

Divide the class into (a) five solo performers and (b) a class chorus. The soloists do a verse each, and the chorus takes over for the italicised parts of the poem. Or, varying small groups of children take on different verses. If the verses are done by soloists, they will need to perform their verses boldly and with confidence, and can either shout out the lines in capital letters or take these lines slowly and softly for emphasis. The soloists can point at the chorus children every time they say the phrase 'I told them'.

Alternatively, the poem could be done by five performers who take a verse each and come together for the chorus parts.

Actions that could be introduced include:

'No, a million birds will fly through me' – wave hands to mimic flight of a bird.

'I'M GOING TO BE A TREE!' – stretch out both arms upright to mimic a tree.

'No, huge whales will swim in me' – hold out both hands as wide as possible.

Feel free to add your own verses – see related writing activity on p. 69.

Overheard on a Saltmarsh

Nymph, nymph, what are your beads?

Green glass, goblin. Why do you stare at them?

Give them me.

        No.

Give them me. Give them me.

           No.

Then I will howl all night in the reeds,
Lie in the mud and howl for them.

Goblin, why do you love them so?

They are better than stars or water,
Better than voices of winds that sing,
Better than any man's fair daughter,
Your green glass beads on a silver ring.

Hush, I stole them out of the moon.

Give me your beads, I want them.

           No.

I will howl in a deep lagoon
For your green glass beads, I love them so.
Give them me. Give them.

        No.

Harold Monro

Performance Notes for 'Overheard on a Saltmarsh'

Teachers can photocopy this poem and use coloured highlight pens to make it clear to children which voices they should adopt – for instance, yellow for the nymph and green for the goblin.

Being a conversation poem, it is most appropriately and effectively performed by two voices, yet rather than simply voicing the words, the two children performing the piece could:

- dress up in costumes
- use props – such as a necklace of glass beads
- consider actions and movements as the piece is performed. Consider – would the nymph be sitting down at first? Would the goblin be following the nymph around? Would the goblin try to snatch the beads away?

Additional children could (a) act as a chorus and add whispering echoes to words such as 'Hush' and 'No' and (b) provide soft, atmospheric music to introduce and conclude the piece.

There is no reason why children could not extend this piece and improvise/write their own additional dialogue and narrative to make this a longer dramatic piece. See related writing activity, p. 68.

Jabberwocky

'Twas brillig, and the slithy toves
   did gyre and gimble in the wabe;
all mimsy were the borogroves,
   and the mome raths outgrabe.

'Beware the Jabberwock, my son!
   The jaws that bite, the claws that catch!
Beware the Jubjub bird, and shun
   The frumious Bandersnatch!'

He took his vorpal sword in hand;
   Long time the manxome foe he sought –
So rested by the Tumtum tree,
   And stood awhile in thought.

And, as in uffish thought he stood,
   The Jabberwock, with eyes of flame,
Came whiffling through the tulgey wood,
   And burbled as it came!

One, two! One, two! And through and through
   The vorpal blade went snicker-snack!
He left it dead, and with its head
   He went galumphing back.

'And hast thou slain the Jabberwock?
   Come to my arms, my bemish boy!
O frabjous day! Callooh! Callay!'
   He chortled in his joy.

'Twas brillig, and the slithy toves
   Did gyre and gimble in the wabe;
All mimsy were the borogroves,
   And the mome raths outgrabe.

Lewis Carroll

Performance Notes for 'Jabberwocky'

A note to teachers who are not familiar with this poem: it does make a lot more sense once you have read it through a few times. Honestly! There is actually a coherent narrative behind the wonderfully bizarre language. For a full interpretation of the poem, see Lewis Carroll's novel *Through the Looking Glass*. The poem appears in the chapter 'Looking-Glass House' and an explanation of the poem is given in the chapter 'Humpty Dumpty'.

There are a number of ways the poem can be performed, including:

- As a rhythmic chant performed by individuals, pairs, a group or the whole class.
- Various verses can be done by individuals/pairs/small groups.
- Because the meaning of the poem is not immediate, the performance needs to help the audience to understand the narrative. To this end, the first verse, which tells of the strange place and the unusual creatures, can be done slowly and with atmosphere.
- Actions will also help to bring out the meaning. Examples:

  'Beware the Jabberwock, my son! – point index finger in the air.
  'The jaws that bite, the claws that catch!' – open mouth wide – and open fingers wide as claws.
  'He took his vorpal sword in hand;' – hold imaginary sword up high.
  'One, two! One, two! And through and through
  The vorpal blade went snicker-snack!' – attack an imaginary beast with an imaginary sword!

One very different way of doing 'Jabberwocky' is to make fun of the strange language, and to perform the poem as a rap. (Thanks to Ewelme C of E Primary School for this idea!) Classes could either (a) do the poem as it is, but perform the piece with an accentuated rap-style rhythm – or (b) classes could perform this new rap version:

Jabberwhatty by James Carter
(a reworking of Lewis Carroll's poem 'Jabberwocky')

Once upon a time in a strange old land
was a little biddy boy with a sword in his hand
and near where he stood by the Tumtum tree
were the weirdest birds you ever did see

Chorus:
Jabber-*whatty?* Jabberwocky!
Jabber-*whatty?* Jabberwocky!
It's a J and an A and a double bubble B
And a this and a that from an A to a Z*

The boy then killed the great Jabberwock
and off with its head he chop-chop-chopped
and that's the tale – no more to say
except for hurrah, callooh, callay!

[Chorus – then repeat the lines:]
and that's the tale – no more to say
except for hurrah, callooh, callay!

* = note: USA pronunciation of 'Z' as in 'zee'!

This version of the poem would work well with a number of voices, and even a whole class. Some children could beatbox along or function as a percussion band. The performance needs to be hearty and lively, and the repeated lines at the end could be brought to a crescendo. Children could swap lines in the chorus – one child/group asks 'Jabber-*whatty?*' and one group replies 'Jabberwocky!'

2

Preparing Poems for Performance

There are a number of stages to work through when preparing for a poetry performance. This section goes through each stage in detail and provides teachers with advice on nurturing poetry performance skills in children.

Think of the control that musicians have over their instruments, as well as the knowledge of the piece that they are playing. Likewise, poetry performers need to have the same degree of control over their voices, and to know every nuance of a poem. But all this takes time, input and a number of rehearsals. The best results will come when performance skills are practised on an ongoing basis, not simply for a one-off poetry concert.

What is important is that children are allowed to bring their own interpretations to a poem and a performance. Everyone has their own individual, subjective response to a piece of writing and children need to be given scope to bring themselves, their experiences and their ideas to poetry in this way.

There is a photocopiable version for children of the teacher's notes that follow on p. 125, entitled 'Stage It'.

Choose It

Choosing the right material is paramount. Performance poems are ones that work well out loud and off the page. The majority of the poems in this book are suitable for performance. And those poems that feature in this chapter each have related performance notes and suggestions.

In addition, there are many poetry anthologies published by Pan Macmillan, Faber & Faber, Oxford University Press, Walker Books, Hodder and others that contain poems ideal for performance. There is a list of recommended poetry collections and anthologies at the back of this book.

For suggestions regarding themed poetry perfromances, see the previous section: 'Staging a Poetry Performance'.

Another worthwhile starting point would be recordings of poems by contemporary children's poets on cassettes/CDs (see 'Recommended Books and CDs'). Classes could listen along to the recordings while reading the printed versions and choose poems they would like to perform themselves. It is important not to be too influenced by the recording, and children must be able to bring their own interpretations to a performance of a piece.

Read It and Learn It

Children will need to read through their chosen poems many times to ensure that they understand each and every word, phrase, line and verse. As Satoshi Kitamura, award-winning illustrator of many children's poetry collections, has commented, it can take a while to really get to know a poem:

> Each poem has its own logic, its own way to be read, which you don't always achieve straight away. This happens to me a lot. And this is both in terms of language, and the rhythm, as well as the content. Not every poem is immediate, it can take a while for you to find the way to read the poem and to appreciate its meaning. Every time a poet writes a new poem, that poem will be a unique world with its own logic and system of language and meaning.

It is important that children are encouraged to ask about any elements of the poem they do not understand or are unsure about.

To be able to give an expressive performance, children will need to learn their poems off by heart. Once children have learnt them, they can then give time to other aspects of performance, such as actions and movement – and how they will give emphasis to certain lines, phrases or words (see 'Note It').

To help them learn their poems, children can work through some of these stages:

- Read the poem to yourself a few times.
- Read the poem out loud with friends.
- Record a reading of the poem onto audio cassette. Listen to it a number of times.
- Think about the poem and recite it quietly to yourself during spare or quiet moments – perhaps before going to sleep or during a journey.

Less confident members of the class may need to keep a copy of the poem with them during a performance; alternatively, one pupil could act as a prompter. Poems written by the children themselves tend to be much more easily learnt by heart.

Note It

Each child will need a photocopy (or two) of the poem on which to make detailed notes.

Classes will require a lot of input as to (a) what to look for and think about when reading through the poem and (b) what specific aspects they can consider when planning a performance.

Here are some pointers to consider when reading through and making notes on a poem:

- Do you like the poem? Why/why not?
- Do you like it more/less the second/third time you read it?
- How does it make you feel?
- Do you think you understand all of the poem?
- What is the poet saying in the poem?
- What is the poem about? Does it tell a story? Does it have a theme/message?
- Does it remind you in any way of any other poem/piece of writing? Why?
- Have you read any other poems by this poet? Is this poem like any others by that poet?
- What form is this poem – a rhyming poem, free verse poem, kenning, haiku, list poem or another form?
- If you were to rewrite this poem, how would you change it?
- Can you think of a different title for the poem?

- Could you write an extra verse or two for the poem?
- Could you write a chorus for the poem?
- What parts could an audience join in with?
- What actions/movements could you do to the poem?
- Is this poem good for performance do you think? Is it a 'page' or a 'stage' poem or both?
- What is the rhythm of the poem? Can you feel the rhythm as you read it out loud? Can you clap along to it? Or does it have a very gentle and subtle rhythm?
- Does it rhyme? Where are the rhyming words? What is the rhyme scheme?
- Can you spot any alliteration/assonance/internal rhymes/half-rhymes?
- Can you spot any similes or metaphors?
- What pictures/images does the poem present?
- What is the mood and tone and atmosphere of the poem?
- Can you count the syllables in each line?
- Is there anything else that you notice about this poem?
- Could you dress up in character for this poem?
- Could you use some props?

For more detailed discussion points on any of the key areas such as rhythm and rhyme, assonance and alliteration or metaphor and imagery, please refer to the relevant sections in the first part of this book.

Before children can interpret a poem in terms of volume/dynamics, pitch, pace, mood/tone, teachers will need to discuss and make notes on each of these key areas beforehand for each poem to be performed:

- *Volume/dynamics* – use soft/loud for specific words/lines/verses; think about how you might whisper some lines, and talk loudly on others. Sometimes, less is more – you can have more impact by whispering a line rather than shouting it. Also think about emphasis, and which words/phrases need to be stressed. For example, consider this line – 'Why are we so afraid of the dark?' Which words should be emphasised? Say the line through, emphasising different words each time. So first '*Why* are we so . . .', second 'Why *are* we so . . .' and so on.
- *Pace* – think of the speed of the poem. Unless it is called for, keep the pace slow to start off with. Could you speed up for effect in certain places? You could slow right down for the very last line – even add an occasional pause for effect – to build excitement, tension and suspense.
- *Rhythm* – if you have chosen a rhythmical and rhyming poem, encourage children not to express the rhythm too mechanically. With free verse poems, the rhythm will be far more subtle, and children may need help discovering how the words should flow. Rhythm is a key area in performance and children will need to experiment with different ways that rhythms of poems can be expressed.
- *Mood/tone* – is it a funny or a serious poem? Is there a range of moods in the piece? Think how you can best express the feeling – and therefore the meaning – of the poem.
- *Pitch* – vary the tone of your voice – high and low, for effect.
- *Pause* – at which points in the poem can you stop to take a breath?

Each of these elements will gradually develop as children work towards a performance, and will come together when they know the poem very well.

The two most problematic areas in performance tend to be volume and pace. Poems so often are said softly and are rushed. Children need to develop their voices so that there is clarity and the poems are said at a reasonable volume – but without children shouting. In most cases, poems will need to be taken slowly. When children start poems at a fast pace they frequently:

- find it hard to sustain throughout
- trip up on certain words
- run out of breath
- lose the meaning/feeling/tone and atmosphere of the poem.

So, just before a performance, children may well need to be reminded to project their voices ('big voice' as teachers frequently say!) and to take their time with the poem.

Share It

Although traditionally poems have in the main been read and performed by individuals, poetry very much lends itself to being performed by a variety of ensembles:

- An *individual* could perform a poem with a chorus (either a group or the whole class) joining in for specific parts. Two poems in this book that would work well in the format: 'Fuss Fuss Fuss' by James Carter and 'You Can't Be That' by Brian Patten. Poems suitable for solo performers would include: 'The Shooting Stars' by James Carter, 'Talking Time' by James Carter, 'The Dark' by James Carter, 'Sorry Sorry Sorry' by James Carter, 'The Visitor' by Valerie Bloom, 'Straining' by Michael Rosen, 'Hedgehog Hiding at Harvest in Hills Above Monmouth' by Helen Dunmore and 'Jabberwocky' by Lewis Carroll.
- *Pairs* of children can chant in unison or swap lines or verses. Poems in this book that would work well by a pair include 'Anansi Meets Big Snake' by Tony Mitton, 'Fireflies' by Paul Fleischman, 'Overheard on a Saltmarsh' by Harold Monro and 'Jabberwocky' by Lewis Carroll.
- In *small groups*, individuals could take a verse or couple of lines each and everyone could come together for the choruses, the final verse or certain lines or phrases for emphasis. Poems in this book suitable for small groups of performers are the same as for *whole class* below.
- A *whole class* can be broken down into smaller groups – perhaps as girls/boys or smaller mixed groups of between four and eight children. (See *individuals* above – backed by whole class.) Poems from this book that are suitable for a whole class performance include: 'Anansi Meets Big Snake' by Tony Mitton, 'Fuss Fuss Fuss' by James Carter, 'Jabberwocky' by Lewis Carroll, 'Red Boots On' by Kit Wright, 'You Can't Be That' by Brian Patten, 'Places in the World' by Red Grammer.

Some children may take the role of *musicians* – and if possible, could play an instrument while performing (such as tambourines, shakers, cabassas) or the class could elect a special group of musicians. (See 'Beat It' below.)

Express It

As part of the 'choreography' of a poem, actions, facial expressions and body movements (and even dances) can be worked out to fit in with certain words, phrases, lines or verses.

Classes can read through their poems and contribute ideas as to what actions, expressions and movements would be appropriate for the pieces. Photocopy versions are useful for making notes on such ideas.

Beat It
Music can be incorporated into the performance of a poem in a number of ways. With more rhythmical poems such as raps and rhyming verse, a small group of children could add a rhythm by using:

- *Parts of the body* to create a beat – hand claps, tapping/stamping feet and beatboxing.
- *Percussion instruments*, for example – cow bells, cabassas, wood blocks, tambourines, shakers and hand drums. If there is a group of percussionists, ensure that the rhythm is (a) quiet so that it does not drown out the words of the poem, and (b) kept very simple, as a complicated rhythm will fight against the rhythm of the poem itself. The instruments must not take over. The poem itself is the most important element, and the volume of the accompaniment must be kept to a minimum during the passages where the children are speaking. One method of using percussion is to only have it feature in certain parts of the poem, such as in the chorus or the final verse. The only way to find out what works best is to improvise and to experiment. If children are to compose a rhythm, this can be recorded onto audio cassette during rehearsals, which will enable the group to assess their performance and also to help them to memorise it.
- A *metronome* – set it to a slow beat to begin with, somewhere between 90 and 98 beats per minute.

Another use of music is to provide atmosphere/tone/mood. This can be achieved by:

- Children composing some instrumental music – on a range of instruments from electronic keyboards to violins, cellos, guitars, percussion instruments such as glockenspiels or xylophones – or even voices producing sound effects. This music could be played at the start of the piece and then could continue very softly throughout the poem, and then could be played again fully at the end.
- Pre-recorded instrumental music – such as film soundtrack music or classical music. The previous David Fulton publication by the author of this very book – *Just Imagine* – features a CD of instrumental music composed especially for creative writing, but would work equally well as introductory pieces to poems.

Classes can even make their own instruments from recycled products such as plastic bottles, rubber bands, cereal packets, tissue boxes and margarine pots. Simple but effective shakers can be made with a sealed container or plastic bottle filled with dried peas, rice or old buttons. Experiment with various contents/quantities of contents so as to produce different sounds.

If you have chosen a rhythmical and rhyming poem, encourage children not to express the rhythm too mechanically. With free verse poems, the rhythm will be far more subtle, and children may need help discovering how the words should flow.

Record It

If a school or class is going to the effort of doing a performance or concert, it is worthwhile recording it onto videotape or audio cassette for posterity.

Recording the rehearsal stages will give instant feedback on what aspects are working well and which areas need further development.

Go For It

You can't hold back in a performance – you have to really go for it!

Nerves are all part of a performance, and children need to be reassured of this. But it is important to have nerves prior to the event, so that when it comes to the performance itself, the nerves will have nearly disappeared. Adrenalin will actually help give energy and vitality to a performance, just so long as the child doesn't say the poem too quickly, which can happen.

Stage It: Performing Poems

Stage It: Performing Poems

CHOOSE IT: find a poem that you really like – one that you enjoy, one that you want to perform. Perhaps you could pick two, and then decide which one you like most.

READ IT AND LEARN IT: get to know the poem really well. Make sure you understand each and every word, phrase and line of the poem. Why not learn the poem off by heart? – if you do, keep a copy of the poem close by in case you need to check the words.

NOTE IT: take a photocopy of the poem and make notes on the page about (a) the sounds and the rhythms of the words/phrases/lines, (b) any ideas you have about performing the poem, and think about:

- *Volume/dynamics* – use soft/loud for specific words/lines/verses, whisper some lines, speak loudly on others.
- *Pace* – think of the speed – keep it slow to start off with – but speed up in certain places? You could slow right down for the very last line – even add an occasional pause – to build excitement, tension and suspense.
- *Rhythm* – what is the rhythm of the poem? Does it change at any point? If you have a rhythmical, rhyming poem try not to say the poem in a mechanical way. Whatever the form or style of poem, experiment with different ways of expressing the rhythm. (See 'Beat It' below)
- *Mood/tone* – is it a funny or serious poem – or is there a range of moods in the piece? Think how you can best express the feeling – and also the meaning – of the poem.
- *Pitch* – high/low, vary the tone of your voice.
- *Pause* – at which points in the poem can you stop to take a breath?

SHARE IT: orchestrate the poem – for example, work out parts for individuals/pairs/groups/the whole class, and decide who will take on specific lines/verses of the poem.

VOICE IT: is the poem written in the voice(s) of a particular character(s)? – if it is, work on how you can capture the voice(s) when you perform the poem.

BEAT IT: clap or tap along if you wish – for all or parts of the poem. Add a percussion track – but keep the rhythm simple and don't let it drown out the words. Even use atmospheric music to open and end the poem.

EXPRESS IT: use actions, facial expressions, body movements, even eye contact.

PROJECT IT: think – is your voice loud (without shouting!) and clear enough – ask others to respond to your rehearsals.

MEAN IT: don't just say the words, mean each and every one of them!

ADD IT: feel free to add a chorus to the poem or write an introduction – make the poem your own.

RECORD IT: to hear how it sounds – and to help you to develop your performance.

ENJOY IT: if you don't, no one else will!

Don't hold back – *Go for it!*

Track Listing for Compact Disc

TRACKS 1–4: poems written and performed by James Carter. Tracks 1 and 4 incorporate music and Track 3 features sound effects.

1: 'The Shooting Stars' – an atmospheric, autobiographical free verse poem (p. 96).
2: 'The Dark' – a playful rhyming poem (p. 98).
3: 'World of Weird' – nonsense rhyming poem (p. 100).
4: 'Electric Guitars' – a playful rhyming poem (p. 102).

TRACKS 5 AND 6: Class 4 (Years 5 and 6) from Ewelme Primary school perform two pieces as a whole class ensemble.

5: 'Places in the World' (by American singer-songwriter Red Grammer) – a song lyric performed as a poem (p. 104).
6: 'Fuss Fuss Fuss or The Goldilocks Rap' (by James Carter) – a rap poem (p. 106).

TRACKS 7 AND 8: two poems written by Year 5 and 6 children from Ewelme Primary School, performed as a whole class ensemble, featuring individual voices.

7: 'Magic in the Moonlight – A Midnight Mystery' – a free verse workshop poem written by Class 4 and James Carter (p. 127).
8: 'The Wonderful World of Doors' – a free verse workshop poem written by Class 4 (p. 129).

TRACK 9: extracts from Shakespeare's play *Macbeth* (Acts I and IV) – performed by three girls from Class 4 at Ewelme C of E Primary School.

9: 'The Witches' (p. 108).

Children's Poems Featured on Compact Disc

The poets from Class 4 of Ewelme (C of E) Primary School in Oxfordshire: Gemma Bolton, Ellie Clements, Connie Jacobs, Lucinda Kenrick, Daniel Miles, Rose Parker, Joanne Phillips, Grace Toland, Francesca Walker, Kit Walker, Elspeth Wilson, Tristan Butler, Eloise Craven-Todd, Jordan Goldspink, Amelia Halhead, Frazer Hunt, Hayley Jameson, Kia Little, Daphne Lloyd, Elizabeth Spence, Rhys Thomas, John Ventress, Elspeth Walker.

Magic in the Moonlight – a Midnight Mystery
by Class 4 of Ewelme (C of E) Primary School with James Carter
(see workshop p. 29 track 7)

Deep in the forest
               there's ƆIƆAM
turning the trees
               silver and gold
twizzling
         and swivelling
               and spinning
                      around

Verse 1

Hush . . .

A lonely wolf waits
   watches
   wonders
   wails

Chorus:

Deep in the forest
    there's MAGIC
mystical – mythical – mischievous
     MAGIC

It follows you
   follows you
     everywhere

Verse 2

HUSH . . .

Creatures crawling
out of who knows where

     Hobbles and Bobbles
     around in a ring
     Thumbles and Boggles
     drifting through air
     hear how they sing

(Chorus)

Verse 3

Hush . . .

A scruffy owl stares
   shrieks
   startles
   swoops invisible

Off to the dark side
    of the forest

(Chorus)

Is it MAGIC
   or madness
     or . . .

The Wonderful World of Doors
by Class 4 of Ewelme C of E Primary School (based on Philip Gross's poem 'The Doors')
(see workshop p. 22/CD track 8)

Down the white corridor
are many different coloured doors

Behind the white door
there is Cloud World
with a sea of snow
pool of ice
waterfall of milk
creamy forests
elegant snowdrops
white doves and silver deer.
All around a marble palace.
A diamond sun, a sapphire sky,
all behind a little white door.

Behind the pale blue door
we found a person,
and she was white and cold,
her skin was icy to touch.
Her eyes were dull and had no sparkle.
Looking round the room,
we saw many different things,
it was just like a doll's house,
then suddenly it dawned on us,
it was one.
The people were porcelain dolls,
that was why they were so silent and still,
we came back out and . . .

One is black and has green eyes
with a bright pink nose
that always shines!
Inside it is a great big room
above you, dusty wooden beams loom.
In the corner are lots of sacks
full to the brim with kittens and cats.
Until you see it, you're never quite sure.
but that's what's behind the cat face door.

Behind the gold and silver door
there is a weird universe
with lots of strange shaped planets
and a planet called maggot world.
Maggot world is a funny place
with maggots, worms and snakes,
poisonous gorillas, man-eating ants,
giant woodlice and monster millipedes.
Maggot world is a funny place
It's weird all around!

Behind the saucy door
all you can see is a town
made out of eatable squishable sauce.
Hot dog men covered in sauce
walking over the ketchup path.
Bricks of houses are made out
of jelly ketchup and mustard.
What do you think?

Behind the camouflage door
is a vulnerable place:
tanks, jeeps, guns and turrets.
War world is a vulnerable place
with mayhem all around.

Behind the candy floss door
there's a magical world of candy.
Chocolate mousses munch
on the caramel rocks
and slurp the trickling flow of fudge.
Jelly babies bounce on the colourful
candy floss clouds.
The orchard of lollypop trees grow on with
everlasting flowers.
That is what's behind the candy floss door.

Behind the black door
with lots of terrifying creatures like
blood sucking bats, scuttling sickening spiders
crawling crusty cockroaches
man eating moths and lurking leeches.
A scruffy screeching owl hoots.

Behind the rainbow-coloured door
is where the rainbow ends.
A weather man looks after all the animals:
red, running rabbits,
orange octopuses eating oranges,
yellow yaks yakking,
green goats eating green grass,
blue bats eating blueberries,
indigo insects in igloos and
violet vultures venturing.
That's what there is
at the end of the rainbow.

Down the white corridor
are many coloured doors.

Watch Out – There's a Poet About

How to Contact Poets and Organise Poetry Events

Having a poet at our school changed the children's concept of poetry and poets. The children were enthralled by the poet's unique approach to writing. (KS2 Literacy Co-ordinator)

The poet's enthusiasm for poetry was infectious. The ideas for inspiring children to write poetry were simple yet very effective. The children thoroughly enjoyed the workshops and staff have found the INSET sessions really worthwhile and very useful. We have plenty of poetry treasures to keep in our pocket for another time! (Headteacher/Year 3 and 4 teacher)

A wonderful afternoon with fantastic ideas for poetry writing. (The poet) helped us to develop our poetry skills and to tap into personal depths of imagination and metaphor, leaving us with real enthusiasm to go back into school with a fresh approach. (Literacy Consultant)

Thank you for sharing your brilliant poems – you really inspired me. (Year 5 girl)

Your poems were fandabadozy! I enjoyed them as much as I enjoy watching Man U score a goal. (Year 6 boy)

There are literally hundreds of poets – including the author of this book! – visiting primary schools all over the UK, and throughout the school year.

The benefits of having a poet in for the day – as I've been told by a great many teachers – are manifold. First, you're getting a specialist in their field – someone who knows about their craft and can discuss all those key areas such as metaphor, rhymes, imagery and drafting. Also, it's someone who can generate a sense of fun with words. And, as teachers regularly introduce us – me and my colleagues are 'real live poets' – people who can demonstrate that books are written by ordinary, everyday people – not mythic beings locked away in ivory towers. We're people who work with words. As one headteacher rightly told me, a visiting writer can also encourage a real community spirit for writing: everyone watches the poet perform together and then gets writing together.

I wouldn't be so daring as to say that a visiting poet can raise literacy standards, but writers can certainly give a sharpened focus to literacy-based work and, above all, raise motivation levels for reading, writing and performing. For me, the best compliment I can be given is to hear a teacher say, 'Robert/Sophie has hardly written a thing all term. Look – s/he wrote a whole page for you!'

What are the Do's and Don'ts?

Make the most of the visit. Get excited about the day. Motivate the children. Read the poet's work before s/he visits. Put enlarged photocopies of the poet's poems on the walls. Have KS1 and KS2 performances in the school hall.

Workshops should have no more than 35 children at a time – and need to be conducted in classrooms with children at their tables. A workshop will need to be at least 45 minutes. I've heard a recent horror story of a poet conducting a workshop in a draughty hall with three Year 1 classes put together all sitting on the floor. I certainly couldn't be creative in those conditions!

A teacher must be present at all times (I've caught a few sneaking off in my time!) and ideally take an active part in the workshops (and yes, some very occasionally choose to do marking, which doesn't send very good signals to the children). Try not to overbook the day – too often poets are invited on the same day as an away football match or the school photographer.

What About National Poetry Day and World Book Day?

- World Book Day: a Thursday in March.
- National Poetry Day: usually falls on the first Thursday in October – as part of Children's Book Week.

Everyone wants a poet on those days – and therefore if you are adamant you need someone at these times you need to book up *at least six months* in advance. If you can't get a poet for those specific days, I advise schools to invite the writer in *before* those days, so that they can come into the school, generate some real enthuasiasm for poetry and get the children writing. And then, on the actual day, the emphasis can ultimately be on the children and their poetry reading, writing and performances.

What About a Poetry/Book Week?

Though they take a lot of organisation – and are best done by two teachers sharing the load – such events really make the most of a literacy-based focus. Schools organise such activities as book quizzes, dressing up as book characters and organising a book fair in the hall after school.

How Much Will It Cost?

Most poets will charge something between £275 and £350 a day – and there will be travelling expenses on top of that. To keep expenses down, you could invite a local poet. Some poets will do half-days, but a whole day will achieve far more. The Poetry Society and some LEAs offer some schemes for funding, often to get a poet to work in a school over a period of time to develop writing skills.

Which Poet Will You Choose?

Factors you may want to consider: Do you want a poet whose work you have been reading in class? Do you want a poet who specialises in a certain form of poetry? Do you want a poet visit to coincide with a specific event? Which year group(s) do you need the author for? Will you be needing a writer who can work with KS1 as well as KS2? Do you want a different poet for KS1 and for KS2? Or do you want someone to work with Gifted and Talented writers in Year 5 all day – or to spend time with Year 6 to get them ready for SATs? But overall, think: What do you want to achieve from the day, and who would be the best to realise this?

Try not to be too specific from the outset – 'I want William Shakespeare for my book week and he must do three workshops and then a performance and then visit the nursery to do some action rhymes and . . .' There is a tendency, the more established the author, the fewer visits they tend to do, so try not to set your heart on acquiring an award-winning or best-selling poet – it could be that they do not do visits any more. And being published does not necessarily guarantee a successful visit. Many excellent and memorable visits are conducted by poets who do not produce books at all – individuals who have a natural gift for performing, running workshops and inspiring young writers.

What Schedule and What to Discuss with the Poet Before the Event

A one-day visit will probably entail one or two performances in the hall. A KS2 performance can be up to 40 minutes, but KS1 need be no more than 20–25 minutes maximum. Some poets, I for one, actually prefer to see Reception and Year 1 together and then put Year 2 in with Years 3 and 4 for performances (depending on the size of the school) – but poets will vary in their preferences.

Leave some time at the end for questions. From there, a poet will conduct up to three or four workshops in the classrooms. Try not to overload the poet – asking the poet to do 20 minutes with each class in a bigger primary school will result in nothing but confused children and a poet in need of a strong coffee. Poets need at least 45 minutes in a classroom to really achieve something with a workshop.

What to Ask When Contacting the Poet

When you first make contact on the phone, ask the poet which age groups s/he writes for and works with and what s/he does in terms of performances and workshops. Rather than stating 'I want a haiku workshop for Year 6, kenning workshop with Year 5 . . .' it is usually best to let the poet run their own tried and tested workshops. However, a poet will be more than happy to oblige a request to discuss the importance of key areas such as drafting or brainstorming. Find out their current publications or ask him/her to send copies of their poems. Many poets will ask to bring their books to sell in the hall at the end of the day – so it is worthwhile sending out slips to parents detailing the titles/costs of the books. It is very helpful if one member of staff can help out at this point – giving change as the poet talks to children/parents and signs books.

Take the poet's address and telephone number (including mobile) and ask if they wish to eat at the school and if they have any dietary requirements. The poet may drive to your school – and if so, will need directions, and if travelling by train may need a lift to and from the station. Finally, ask the poet if they have any specific requirements – for example, that classes write on mini-white boards or they need access to a power point. On arrival, the poet will need the schedule for the day, a brief tour, an introduction to the head and the staff and will need to be shown the staff room and the loo.

Some poets will also do performances and/or talks or workshops for parents and staff after school hours – as well as INSET sessions – but these are best held on separate days to school visits.

What About a Residency?

A series of visits/residency from a poet will allow him/her to meet more classes or even do an extended project with one or two classes. This will give the poet time to properly address such issues as drafting and brainstorming, and developing poems, to explore further the nature and forms of poetry, to get to know interests and ability levels, and to conduct a range of different workshops and to work towards a rehearsed performance of the children's own writing.

What Should I Get from a Visit?

Well, a good visit from a poet is, indirectly, an INSET session on how to write, perform, share and enjoy poetry with others. In the workshops, the poets will give teachers a wealth of ideas for their own future poetry writing workshops. Hopefully, the whole school will have a real buzz afterwards – and feel really positive about the visit, and be keen to carry on writing, reading and performing poetry. Afterwards, why not get together in the staffroom to brainstorm activities that you liked? Poets often do different workshops in the various classes – so you could pass around some of the poems your class has written. Also share any of the tips the writer has. Tell other teachers from other schools about the day. Spread the word!

A worthwhile visit will work on many levels, and children will react in different ways. Some children will enjoy the performance most and get a great deal from seeing how poetry can come to life. Other children will get more from the workshop and enjoy sharing their writing with the poet or asking questions about the writing process or getting published. Please note that children do not necessarily write their best pieces during the poet's visit. Some children feel intimidated writing in front of a published poet/stranger, and may be inspired in other ways – to want to go on and read some poems, to learn some, to look for poetry books at home or down at the library.

How Can I Make the Most of the Day?

Exploit it for what it's worth. Ensure the visit is part of a continuum, a process. Work on poetry, especially that poet's writing, before the day. Get the children thinking of general and specific questions they can ask the poet. Listen attentively during the performance so you can discuss certain poems with the children later. Make notes during the workshops. The very best performances and workshops are, without exception, where the teachers are 100 per cent committed and involved. And why not ask two child volunteers to read out their own poems – previously written – to the poet on the day? Children love doing this. Afterwards, the children can craft and draft their poems. Perhaps they can write more poems based on some of the poet's own work. Make displays of the poems – publish them in *Young Writer* magazine or at Poetryzone website (see below). Why not ask the class to write to the poet? Most poets are more than happy to reply with a generic response to the class.

Should I Make This Part of the School Calendar?

Why not? Some schools invite in a different poet every year. Some rotate a poet/fiction writer/illustrator or even a drama/dance/music group every three years. Those schools that have an annual topic-based week – say a science week, arts week or book week – invite a writer related to that topic. Or you could ask a poet in to write some science-based poems, or poems in response to the children's art work.

In What Other Ways Can We Celebrate Poetry?

Here a just a few fun poetry activities:

- make a poetry tree ('poetree') of children's favourite poets/poems;
- put up poems all over the school (even the loo!) – enlarge them on the photocopier: from shape poems to haikus, raps to free verse – all sorts;
- listen to tapes of poets reading their poems (and ask the children to record theirs too);
- KS2 children visit KS1 classes to read their own poems – or vice versa;
- write a class poem – every child writes a line or a verse each, then perform the poem in a long 'conga' line;
- write a class or school rap;
- have a poetry performance/assembly;
- teachers rotate around the classes *performing* (not just reading!) a favourite poem;
- publish poems in class anthologies/school magazine or website;
- invite local media – radio and local newspaper – to cover the event.

Where Can You Get a Poet From?

A variety of places:

- Poetryzone website (it's fantastic) at www.poetryzone.ndirect.co.uk;
- The Travelling Book Company (freefone 0800 731 5758) – the company also organises nationwide school book fairs;
- the agency Speaking of Books (020 8692 4704);
- the Poetry Society (020 7420 9892);
- children's poetry publishers – such as Pan Macmillan (020 7833 4000) and Walker Books (020 7793 0909) – ask for the publicity departments;
- ask other local schools if they have any recommendations; don't worry if you haven't heard of the poet before – some of the very best poetry performers and workshop leaders are not household names;
- NAWE – National Association of Writers in Education – they have an extensive database of poets and all kinds of writers and illustrators at their website – www.nawe.co.uk;
- go to a library/bookshop or read a current magazine such as *Books for Keeps* or *Carousel* or *School Librarian* to see which poets are currently being published, to give you some ideas.

Recommended Books and CDs

Books on Poetry and Creative Writing

Just Imagine: Creative Ideas for Writing – James Carter (David Fulton) – creative writing manual – book/CD for KS2.

Talking Books – James Carter (RoutledgeFalmer) – a book of interviews with children's authors from Jacqueline Wilson to Philip Pullman, Terry Deary to Benjamin Zephaniah.

To Rhyme or Not to Rhyme? – Sandy Brownjohn (Hodder & Stoughton).

Black's Rhyming and Spelling Dictionary – Pie Corbett and Ruth Thompson (A&C Black).

Writing Poetry at KS3 – Pie Corbett (David Fulton) – many workshops apropriate to KS2.

Poetry in the Making – Ted Hughes (Faber & Faber).

Rose, Where Did You Get That Red? Teaching Great Poetry to Children – Kenneth Koch (Vintage).

Wishes, Dreams and Lies: Teaching Children to Write Poetry – Kenneth Koch (HarperCollins).

Catapults and Kingfishers – Brian Moses and Pie Corbett (Oxford University Press).

So You Want To Write Poetry – Brian Moses (Hodder Wayland).

Did I Hear You Write? – Michael Rosen (Andre Deutsch).

Read My Mind: Young Children, Poetry and Learning – Fred Sedgwick (RoutledgeFalmer).

The Poetry Book for Primary Schools – ed. by Anthony Wilson (The Poetry Society).

Writers' and Artists' Yearbook (Pan Macmillan) – updated annually.

And dictionaries, dictionaries, dictionaries – children need access to words, words, words to develop their vocabularies – and try encyclopedias too!

Poetry Anthologies

Under the Moon and Over the Sea: Caribbean Poems – John Agard and Grace Nichols (Walker Books).

This Poem Doesn't Rhyme – Gerard Benson (Puffin).

One River Many Creeks: Poems from Around the World – Valerie Bloom (Pan Macmillan).

The Apple Raid: Poems for Year 3/4/5 Pie Corbett (Pan Macmillan).

What Shape Is a Poem? – Paul Cookson (Pan Macmiilan).

The Works 1 – Paul Cookson (Pan Macmillan).

The Works 2 – Pie Corbett and Brian Moses (Pan Macmillan).

The Works 3 – Paul Cookson (Pan Macmillan).

Overheard on a Saltmarsh – Carol Ann Duffy (Young Picador).

My First Oxford Book of Poems – John Foster (Oxford University Press).

101 Favourite Poems – John Foster (Collins).

The Ring of Words – Roger McGough (Faber & Faber).

Sensational Poems Inspired by the Five Senses – Roger McGough (Pan Macmillan)

The Kingfisher Book of Poems About Love – Roger McGough (Kingfisher).

Read Me 1 and 2 – Gaby Morgan (Pan Macmillan).

The Secret Lives of Teachers: The School Year – Brian Moses (Pan Macmillan).

Poems Out Loud – Brian Moses (Hodder Wayland) – CD/book

Hysterical Historical Poems (Hodder Wayland) – a series of books.

Hubble Bubble: Magic Poems – Andrew Fusek Peters (Hodder Wayland).

The Puffin Book of Utterly Brilliant Poetry – Brian Patten (Puffin).

Puffin Book of Twentieth Century Children's Verse – Brian Patten (Puffin).

Classic Poetry: An Illustrated Collection – Michael Rosen (Walker Books).

The Faber Book of Children's Verse – Matthew Sweeney (Faber & Faber).

Talking Drums – Veronique Tadjo (A & C Black).

Poetry Collections

Hello H20/Einstein, The Girl Who Hated Maths – John Agard (Hodder Wayland).

Please Mrs Butler/Heard It In the Playground/Friendly Matches – Allan Ahlberg (Puffin).

Playing a Dazzler/When I Dance – James Berry (Hamilton).

Whoop an' Shout!/Hot Like Fire – Valerie Bloom (Macmillan).

The World is Sweet – Valerie Bloom (Bloomsbury).

Cars Stars Electric Guitars – James Carter (Walker Books).

Collected Poems for Children – Charles Causley (Macmillan).

Revolting Rhymes/Dirty Beasts – Roald Dahl (Puffin).

Wallpapering the Cat – Jan Dean (Pan Macmillan).

Walking on Air – Berlie Doherty (Collins).

Picture a Poem – Gina Douthwaite (Red Fox).

Meeting Midnight/The Oldest Girl In The World – Carol Ann Duffy (Faber & Faber).

Snollygoster – Helen Dunmore (Scholastic).

Joyful Noise: Poems for Two Voices – Paul Fleischman (HarperCollins USA).

Big Talk: Poems for Four Voices – Paul Fleischman (Walker Books).

You Little Monkey!/Making Waves/Standing on the Sidelines/Doctor Proctor/Four o'Clock Friday – John Foster (Oxford University Press).

Manifold Manor – Philip Gross (Faber & Faber).

My Dog Is a Carrot – John Hegley (Walker Books).

The Pedalling Man – Russell Hoban (Hodder).

The Curse of the Vampire's Socks – Terry Jones (Puffin).

The Frog Who Dreamed She Was an Opera Singer – Jackie Kay (Bloomsbury).

Two's Company – Jackie Kay (Puffin).

Bad Bad Cats/Pie in the Sky – Roger McGough (Puffin).

The Complete Edward Lear (Faber & Faber).

The Very Best of . . . Ian McMillan (Macmillan).

Plum/Red and White Spotted Handkerchief/Fluff/Tale of Tales – Tony Mitton (Scholastic).

Various Rap collections – Tony Mitton (Orchard Books).

Don't Look at Me In That Tone of Voice/Barking Back at Dogs – Brian Moses (Macmillan).

Collected Poems for Children – Gareth Owen (Macmillan).

Juggling with Gerbils/Gargling with Jelly – Brian Patten (Puffin).

Choose Your Superhero – Norman Silver (Hodder).

Where the Sidewalk Ends – Shel Silverstein (Puffin).

The Monster That Ate the Universe/I Did Not Eat the Goldfish – Roger Stevens (Pan Macmillan).

The Journal of Danny Chaucer (Poet) – Roger Stevens (Orion).

A Garden of Verses – Robert Louis Stevenson (Puffin).

Wouldn't You Like to Know/Mind Your Own Business/Don't Put Mustard in the Custard – Michael Rosen (Scholastic).

Centrally Heated Knickers – Michael Rosen (Puffin).

You Tell Me – Michael Rosen and Roger McGough (Puffin).

Up On The Roof/Fatso in the Red Suit – Matthew Sweeney (Faber & Faber).

The Poetical Works of Phoebe Flood – John Whitworth (Hodder).

Cat Among the Pigeons/Hot Dog – Kit Wright (Puffin).

Talking Turkeys/Funky Chickens – Benjamin Zephaniah (Puffin).

Poets who record their poems for cassettes/CDs are: Roger McGough, Brian Patten, Michael Rosen, Brian Moses and Valerie Bloom.

The anthology CD *Poems Out Loud* (presented by Brian Moses) listed above is also a good introduction to children's poetry and features many performance poets – including Michael Rosen, John Agard, Brian Moses, Valerie Bloom and Pie Corbett.